Sidelights on the American Revolution

Sidelights on the American Revolution

Webb Garrison

Abingdon Press
Nashville · New York

Sidelights on the American Revolution

Copyright © 1974 by Abingdon Press

Library of Congress Cataloging in Publication Data

GARRISON, WEBB B
  Sidelights on the American Revolution. Nashville, Abingdon Press,
  Bibliography: p. 1974.
  1. United States—History—Revolution, 1775–1783—Anecdotes. I. Title.
E296.G26   973.3   74-10981

176 p.
22 cm.

E
296
G26

ISBN-0-687-38439-7

MANUFACTURED BY THE PARTHENON PRESS AT
NASHVILLE, TENNESSEE, UNITED STATES OF AMERICA

To Mary

for constant inspiration
and a ceaseless source of ideas

Introduction

Most of the principal characters in the unfolding drama of the American Revolution have been depicted in detail. So have their roles and the backgrounds against which those roles were played.

But because the historian is continually required to sift and choose, deleting many things that are less important than others, no account of so broad a stretch of time as that included in the traditional revolutionary years can possibly be complete. Necessity for getting on with the story requires that the person framing a comprehensive account must leave out many a person, place, and event.

This volume makes no attempt to provide a capsule account of the entire story of the Revolution. It comes to focus, instead, upon byways of history. A hasty decision for the sake of political expediency mushrooms into national policy. Motives never fully explained cause a man to shoot—or not to shoot—and the long-range import of his spur of the moment decision affects the whole Western world.

Because any history, in the words of Henry Steele Commager, must begin somewhere and come to a clear-cut ending at a precise time and place, the American Revolution is traditionally treated as having taken place between December 16, 1773, and September 3, 1783. The places involved on these dates are, respectively, Boston and Paris. The events on these dates are the unlawful dumping of merchandise belonging to the East India Company into Boston harbor and the affixing of signatures to a definitive treaty of peace between Great Britain and the United States of America.

Convenient as these boundaries are—indeed, essential as they are to an account that must begin and end somewhere—adoption of them represents a vast oversimplification. The time sequence and geographical expanse of the Revolution are far vaster than conventional dates and places suggest. Events (and the persons who helped to shape those events) that took place long, long before the Boston Tea Party helped set the stage for a conflict that was interminably slow in coming but was as inevitable as the eventual thud of a stone flung into the sky by one who has great strength but no target.

Consequently, this volume ranges far and wide—in time as well as space. In vignette form, it deals with some persons and places and events that—at first look—seem to have little to do with the British-American strife along the eastern seaboard of North America during the decade that began in December, 1773.

Because it is a round-up of the unusual and the relatively unknown, this collection of vignettes does not fall neatly into a set of chapters with clearly defined subjects. Instead it ranges from notice of the great chain with which patriots tried to block British access to the Hudson river to a fighting Continental whose battlefield exploits were overshadowed by horticultural ones that made his name a household word. Since most Americans tend to think of the Revolution as having involved North American colonists and armed invaders of these shores, roles played by British and European leaders are often minimized. As a corrective to this historical astigmatism, considerable emphasis is here placed upon persons—some famous in other contexts, many all but forgotten in America—who, from a distance of three thousand miles or more helped to form the warp and woof of the War of Independence.

Some of our most widely known and highly cherished traditions about the Revolution are plainly mythical; here and there, in these pages, the pin of truth pricks the balloon of fancy. But on the other side of the coin, some of the little things on which battles or legislation turned—or even the outcome of the struggle itself—are treated in a fashion that is impossible when one seeks to deal with every major campaign and issue and all leading personalities.

While presented as a fun book, every effort has been made to prepare here a volume that will also serve as a useful reference tool. To that end, an exhaustive index is included.

May these pages bring you that indefinable but real experience of being surprised by joy as you look at the American Revolution from a new perspective and discover or rediscover that the most momentous of events often take their shape from the shadows of other things frequently entirely overlooked or given only a passing glance.

WEBB GARRISON

On the Banks of the Ohio
Spring, 1974

Contents

Thunder and Lightning

Patrick Henry to the Rescue

Patrick Henry is remembered chiefly for his famous "Give me liberty, or give me death!" speech. Long before that, however, he went to the rescue of colonists who felt themselves injured by legal decisions in Britain.

For generations, the Anglican clergy of Virginia were paid with tobacco rather than with gold or silver. Law stipulated that each priest was to receive 16,000 pounds of tobacco per year. In practice, the clergy settled for papers representing certificates that tobacco was safely stored in warehouses waiting for shipment to England.

This system worked reasonably well during typical years, for the economy of Virginia was based upon tobacco. But during the early 1750s a succession of crop failures led to a sharp rise in the price of the leaf. To deal with the problem created by payment of clergy in terms of tobacco, in 1755 and in 1758 the Virginia Assembly passed the Two-Penny Acts. These statutes stipulated that clergymen were to be paid for their 16,000 pounds of tobacco at two pence per pound—well below the market value.

Angry priests and their supporters took the case to England, where in early 1763 judges declared the Two-Penny Acts null and void. This provided a foundation on which the Reverend James Maury could bring suit for damages and have every reason to expect to collect. But when the hearing began in November, 1763, the defendants (Assemblymen of the Colony of Virginia) retained as their counsel twenty-seven-year-old Patrick Henry. Henry's impassioned defense included a fiery attack upon the British monarch which brought cries of "Treason! Treason!" from assembled listeners. But when the jury returned its verdict, defendants were ordered to pay James Maury damages in the sum of precisely one penny.

England's War Debt

The Peace of Paris, 1763, ended the Seven Years' War—in which England and France had fought against one another on both sides of the Atlantic. But the restoration of peace meant the beginning of new troubles for England's leaders. War debts (part of them brought on by the French and Indian War in the New World) had caused the British Treasury to reach a deficit of £136,000,000.

More than any other single factor, it was the war debt of England that caused lawmakers to seek new sources of revenue, which eventually produced a series of fiscal measures that collectively became known in the colonies as the Intolerable Acts.

The well-known Stamp Act of 1765 actually represented a fairly routine attempt to create new revenue. In the mother country, it had long been an accepted practice that revenue stamps had to be affixed to many kinds of legal papers. This practice is now followed not only in the United States, but in most other highly developed countries.

North American reaction was quick and violent, however. The Stamp Act Congress which met in New York in October, 1765, had representatives from nine of the thirteen colonies. Here the delegates gave the nod to a petition—properly subservient in its language toward the king—that established the principle that no taxes should be imposed in the colonies without consent of citizens there.

For practical purposes, American reaction to the revenue-raising procedures of which the Stamp Act was symbolic amounted to a flat repudiation of the authority of Parliament. Reaction actually reached such a level that the Stamp Act had to be repealed, But the war debt remained, and it was the job of England's national leaders to try to liquidate it. Their only source of new revenue was the colonies, so the debt put England on a collision course with her loyal subjects three thousand miles away.

First Martyr of the Revolution

Massachusetts—early seedbed of trouble—experienced violence and death long before the famous tea party or the Battles of Lexington and Concord. The first authenticated account of an American martyr appeared in the *Boston Evening Post* on February 26, 1770. The victim was eleven-year-old Christopher Snider.

Tempers were already running high in the port city. Many merchants had signed an agreement that they would no longer import articles of British manufacture or goods transported in British ships. Other merchants—some because of loyalist leanings and others for the sake of potential profit—had refused to sign the agreement.

Angry patriots placed markers against the houses of those merchants who refused to take the hard line of economic resistance to Britain. But equally angry sympathizers of the loyalist cause reacted by removing these markers. Ebenezer Richardson was generally believed to have been the man who took down the markers that had been set against the house of his neighbor, Theophilus Lille.

A mob gathered to reprimand Richardson, and perhaps to toss him in a blanket. He reacted by grabbing his musket and shooting at random. He hit Sammy Gore, whose wound was not mortal. But the sight of blood set patriots on fire; they charged against the home of Richardson who continued to fire as rapidly as he could. Before the fracas was over, eleven-year-old Christopher Snider lay dead—a victim of economic and patriotic passions that were to produce a revolution. Convicted of murder, Richardson drew an extremely light sentence, just two years in jail.

A Stout Man with a Cord Wood Stick

Crispus Attucks, one of three Boston citizens killed by the British volley that has gone down in history as the Boston Massacre, is noted as "the first to defy, and the first to die."

Though he figured prominently in the clash between patriots and soldiers of the army of occupation and was a major figure in the trial of British commander Captain Thomas Preston, hardly anything is known about him.

Probably correctly, present-day black historians insist that Attucks was black. Earlier authorities have identified him both as an Indian of the Natick tribe and as a mulatto of mixed Indian and Negro blood.

The case for Attucks' place in black history rests largely upon an advertisement in the *Boston Gazette*. On October 2, November 13, and November 20, 1750 (a full twenty years before the massacre), Deacon William Browne of Framingham, Massachusetts, advertised for his runaway slave. Browne described him as "a mulatto fellow, about 27 years of age, named Crispus, 6 feet 2 inches high, short, curl'd hair, his knees nearer together than common."

The dark-skinned victim of British gunfire on March 5, 1770, was unusually big. Witness after witness testified to his size and color. But no one had clear information about his race or background. The distinguished *Dictionary of American Biography* ventures to guess that "It is possible that he was a sailor on a whaling ship."

Boston selectman Oliver Wendell testified that "a stout man with a cord wood stick" whom he believed to be "the mulatto" grabbed a British bayonet with one hand and wielded his stick with the other. Beyond this, and the fact that he died as a result of the first volley fired by the British, virtually nothing is certain about Revolutionary hero Crispus Attucks.

Paul Revere, Propagandist

Paul Revere's influence as a courier, universally known, actually was not nearly so important as his role as a propagandist. One of his engravings was one of the most widely circulated pieces of propaganda of the era, and it helped to precipitate the actual revolution.

The famous coppersmith called his work "THE BLOODY MASSACRE perpetrated in King Street BOSTON on March 5th 1770 by a party of the 29th REG."

Revere's engraving of the Boston Massacre depicts Captain Preston—sword drawn—giving the command to fire. In response to that command, muskets of British soldiers blaze into an orderly and respectable crowd of citizens, in front of whom the dead and wounded lie in the street.

Eighteen lines of verse beneath the engraving declare that savage bands (of British)

> With murd'rous Rancour stretch their bloody hands,
> Like fierce Barbarians grinning o'er their Prey

and conclude with the warning that

> Should venal courts, the scandal of the land,
> Snatch the relentless villain from her hand,
> Keen execrations, on this plate inscribed,
> Shall reach a judge who never can be bribed.

Revere's engraving, supported by little evidence from eye-witnesses, served to catch the eyes and to inflame the passions of most Americans who saw it. Few propagandists of any era have done a better job than did Revere, whose exaggerated and greatly distorted interpretation became accepted as cold fact.

John Adams, Attorney for the Defense

On September 7, 1770, the attention of Boston—and much of Massachusetts—focused on the Boston Town House. Captain Thomas Preston, British officer of the day on March 5, was going on trial for his life.

It was Preston, popular opinion asserted, who was responsible for the Boston Massacre that had inflamed the entire northeastern section of Britain's North American empire. Only hours after the shooting incident, Governor Thomas Hutchinson launched a formal inquiry. Witnesses were examined by Justices of the Peace Richard Dana and John Tudor.

As evidence mounted, an official decision was reached at 2:00 A.M. March 6. Acting on a writ issued by the court, the sheriff went to arrest Captain Preston. By 3:00 A.M. he was lodged in jail.

Preston, who vowed from the beginning that he had never ordered his men to fire, was sure he could not get a good attorney to defend him. Still, he persuaded James Forrest—a huge fellow nicknamed "the Irish infant"—to try to get help. Forrest got a conditional acceptance from fledgling lawyer Josiah Quincy. Yes, Quincy would engage to defend the captain on one provision—that his relative, the distinguished John Adams, must join him on the case.

Adams listened to the plea of Forrest. Already, he was sure that evidence against Captain Preston was heavily weighted by emotion. He accepted one guinea as a retainer to seal the agreement and became the chief defender of the man charged with having started the Boston Massacre.

Court opened on September 7. Preston's superior officers and most of his friends had deserted him. But a brilliant defense, including firsthand testimony from eyewitnesses, brought a quick acquital. Thanking his attorney, Preston had no idea that he was indebted to a man destined to become the second President of the republic not yet formed.

Jonathan Shipley, Bishop of St. Asaph

Since the Church of England was (and is) the official religious body of England, bishops had great political influence. Inevitably, this meant that a man being considered for elevation to the office was closely scrutinized by the king and his ministers.

Jonathan Shipley, born in 1714, was consecrated as bishop in 1769 and during the same year was moved to a larger and more prominent see (or area of responsibility). Historians who view events of the period from a distance take this as "sure evidence" that Shipley was then in high favor with the king.

Soon after his elevation to the high office, however, he began to show some signs of sympathy for Whig doctrines. It was his reputation for open-mindedness in this respect that led Benjamin Franklin to seek him out in 1771. The two men quickly developed a warm spirit of rapport. Franklin wrote home about the "sweet air of Twyford" (episcopal residence of Shipley). Shipley, meanwhile, did his best to introduce Franklin to men of influence—regardless of their political views. More than any other Englishman, it was the Anglican bishop who made the American printer-scientist-philosopher a notable figure in Britain.

Writing in May, 1774, in opposition to the Massachusetts Government Act (denying Massachusett's charter), the Bishop of St. Asaph said to fellow leaders of the church: "My Lords, I look upon North America as the only great nursery of freemen now left upon the face of the earth." He appealed for their support, but got that of only one man—Hinchlifee, Bishop of Peterborough.

Shipley was Franklin's closest friend in Europe. It was at Twyford that Franklin wrote part of his *Autobiography*. Shipley boosted the American to prominence in Britain—and as a result lost his own chance to become Archbishop of Canterbury, head of the Anglican Church.

The Navigation Acts

England's first set of Laws of Trade and Navigation—popularly called Navigation Acts—was enacted in 1651. On the surface, the legislation would seem to be far removed from the conflict that erupted 125 years later. Actually, these statutes represented the first steps along a path that was inevitably to lead to revolution.

The Navigation Acts at first prescribed conditions under which goods from British colonies in Africa, Asia, and America could be transported to the island kingdom. Largely in an attempt to hurt the Dutch, it was decreed that prescribed cargoes could be transported only in English vessels.

Just nine years after the first of the Navigation Acts was put into force Parliament added teeth to the measure and greatly expanded it. All foreign ships—of whatever nation—were forbidden to transport goods to or from English colonies or to engage in trade with them. Colonists were forbidden to ship certain raw materials to any destination other than England. Tobacco, sugar, and cotton were on the list from the beginning; later rice, molasses, furs, and naval stores were added.

The effect of the series of Navigation Acts was to create a monopoly for the benefit of English merchants and shippers. Colonists were forbidden to purchase directly from foreign sources. If goods originated in a Spanish or a French region, they had to go to England for payment of duty before they could be transshipped to the colonies—at higher prices.

As the backbone of England's colonial policy, the Navigation Acts created increasingly burdensome conditions in all regions where Britain had outposts. Only in the New World was opposition sufficiently vocal and organized to set once-loyal subjects to firing muskets at the king's soldiers in the 1770s.

Abraham Whipple Takes the *Gaspeé*

Almost eighteen months before the universally well-known Boston Tea Party, anti-British zealots carried out a far more daring and colorful exploit.

The Colonial packet *Hannah,* loaded with contraband merchandise that was being smuggled into the country, was sighted by the British schooner *Gaspée.* A twenty-five-mile chase ensued, with the *Gaspée* failing to succeed in catching the *Hannah.* Off the coast of Rhode Island, the *Gaspée* ran aground, and the *Hannah* continued her interrupted voyage certain to bring substantial illegal profits to those who had invested in her.

Matters should have ended at that point, had common sense prevailed. But seamen of the New England coast had abandoned common sense long ago. They were ready and eager to strike a blow against the hated customs officials and the ships that (ineffectually) tried to enforce the law of the land.

On the evening of June 6, 1772, eight longboats led by Captain Abraham Whipple boarded and captured the British gunboat. They took British seamen to Pawtuxet and turned them loose —but they burned the *Gaspée.* The British crown offered huge rewards and immunity to informers. A special commission sat from January to June, 1773, but no participant in the raid was ever captured.

Logically, this armed assault upon a gunboat of His Majesty's Navy should have provoked much sterner reprisal than the dumping of tea into Boston harbor. But in 1772 sentiment in Britain was still heavily in favor of conciliation, so loss of the naval vessel went unpunished.

Boston Tea Cheaper Than in England

The Boston Tea Party, December 16, 1773, is considered by many historians to be the overt incident that marked the beginning of violent revolution. From today's perspective it seems strange since the tea dumped into Boston Harbor by Paul Revere, John Hancock, and about one hundred other patriots disguised as American Indians was substantially cheaper than the same tea sold in England.

Two sets of factors contributed to the paradoxical situation.

England's famous East India Company, for whom tea was a staple in trade, faced financial ruin. It was imperative that the company be not only permitted but encouraged to do business in North America—where the monopoly on tea was total. To encourage trade, on May 10, 1773, Parliament enacted a statute permitting the Company to export tea to the colonies "with remission of ordinary British duties."

But in this situation, King George vehemently insisted upon maintaining "a peppercorn of a principle." Since other obnoxious taxes had been dropped, the monarch feared that failure to collect token duty on tea would weaken the power to tax in the future. "There must always be one tax to keep up the right"was the principle upon which he operated. Over strenuous objections, the king's insistence led to imposition of an import duty of three pence per pound on tea taken directly to North America —bypassing British middle men, hence eliminating their profit.

Tea dumped into Boston harbor was to have been placed on the market at prices substantially lower than the same tea could have been bought by His Majesty's loyal subjects in London or Coventry or Salisbury or any other city in the British Isles. So it was not consumer price, but the "very principle of taxation" to which the Sons of Liberty violently objected.

A Former Tax Collector Fights Taxation

.

On the night of the famous Boston Tea Party, one of the happiest men in the colony was Samuel Adams. No one knows whether he personally participated in dumping the taxed tea into the ocean. But it is clear from records of the era that the "Committees of Correspondence" that he formed with the aid of Joseph Warren beginning on November 2, 1772, were responsible for the flagrant insult to the British crown.

Adams, a superpatriot often called "The Great Agitator," had more than ordinary knowledge of taxes.

Descended from a patrician Boston family and a graduate of Harvard, he knew how to manage political movements but never succeeded in managing his own affairs with success. He worked briefly in the countinghouse of Thomas Cushing after graduating from Harvard, then left to set up his own business. He failed in a few months, then joined his father in running the family brewery. After his father's death, Sam quickly ran through his share of the estate.

That's why, in 1756, the blue-blooded Adams took the job of tax collector for Boston. He remained in the post eight years before being ousted because he owed the town £8,000 in back taxes.

Some letters and documents indicate that Samuel Adams was ardently advocating active rebellion as early 1768. In any case, the one-time tax collector became an eloquent critic of British taxation. Though he was perpetually in financial trouble, his pamphlets and speeches placed him in the front rank of men responsible for arousing sentiment that led to armed revolution.

Paul Revere's Forgotten Rides

Silversmith-engraver-patriot Paul Revere took to the saddle at least as early as the winter of 1773. During that season, he rode all the way to New York City to notify the Sons of Liberty that a tea party was being planned in Boston. A few months later, when Boston was made the target of the Boston Port Bill, he went to both New York and to Philadelphia to get help for the beleaguered city.

Paul Revere rode to Philadelphia once more in 1774, bearing a copy of the admittedly subversive "Suffolk Resolves"—a set of resolutions enacted in defiance of Britain's Intolerable Acts. In December of the same year he galloped most of the night in order to reach the home of John Sullivan on the Oyster River (near Portsmouth). This time, he bore warning that General Gage planned to seize the little fortress of William and Mary —significant chiefly because it held "a good store of powder." Revere's message reached patriots in time, they seized enough powder and shot to cover their retreat at Bunker Hill six months later.

Historian Stewart Holbrook goes so far as to declare that the ride made famous by Henry W. Longfellow was "the least important of all Revere's many rides." That is probably an exaggeration, but few Americans know that the name of Paul Revere frequently appeared in London newspapers before he made his short but famous "midnight ride."

Far from modest, Paul Revere himself several times told various versions of his many rides made in the name of liberty. His account of the journey made on the night of April 18, with a prearranged signal of "two lanthorns in the North Church steeple [if the British went by water]; and if by land, one," so impressed Longfellow that the poet chose this occasion as the subject of his famous poem.

Pine Tar and Goose Feathers

In those communities where Whigs (or patriots) were in the majority, Tories (or loyalists) were threatened with physical harm as well as with loss of their civil rights in the turbulent era before full-fledged war broke out.

Native Bostonian John Malcolm, a wealthy veteran of the French and Indian Wars who had turned against his countrymen by becoming a customs official, began to receive threats as early as November, 1773. He ignored them and went about his business.

On January 25, 1774, a band of Whigs broke into Malcolm's house. Though he was armed, they seized him and put him on a sled which they drew to the Customs House. There the patriots stripped the symbol of royal authority "to buff and breeches" and gave him a liberal dose of pine tar plus goose feathers.

Later this treatment of Tories became so common that patriots circulated a recipe for administering the two substances to the bodies of England's supporters.

Malcolm, who later claimed (perhaps correctly) to be the first American to be treated with tar and feathers because of his political views, was ordered to curse the governor of Massachusetts. He refused several times. Eventually the crowd dragged him to the town gallows and gave him the option of cursing the governor or having his ears cut off.

He submitted, cursed the governor aloud and the patriots silently, and spent five days in bed nursing his injuries before he was strong enough to dictate a letter of complaint to Governor Hutchinson. The tar and feathers peeled off with much of his skin still adhering to it; he took one piece to England in May where he unsuccessfully tried to get compensation for injuries he suffered at the hands of patriots.

Six Aristocrats Cool a Hot Potato

Word of the Boston Tea Party reached London late in January, 1774. On one point practically all persons in positions of authority were agreed: something would have to be done; the matter could not be ignored. But precisely what should be done was a question that was not readily answered. General Thomas Gage, commander of British forces in North America, was home on leave. Questioned by the king himself, Gage urged caution. A military solution was not necessarily the answer, he said. "While we're lambs, [inflamed rebels] will be lions."

Gage had no opportunity to have a voice in the final decision about response to "a raid by a band of Mohawk Indians" upon tea ships of the East India Company.

The North American question was handed to the British Cabinet. Only six men—all aristocrats—attended the meeting at the Whitehall Street office of Lord Rocheford, a secretary of state for overseas affairs.

Minutes of the meeting indicate that an unidentified lord quipped: "We are meeting on an unlucky day, Friday; we must be careful how we cool this hot potato."

At least one man—Lord Sandwich, First Lord of the Admiralty—was cool to the idea of punitive action three thousand miles from home. But under the urging of the Earl of Dartmouth, who was Secretary for the Colonies, the six assembled aristocrats who comprised the cabinet meeting arrived at concensus. Boston's harbor would be closed. "Four or five frigates will do the business," Lord North later said in the House of Commons.

The punishment would be severe—but could be modified as soon as the repentant Americans paid for tea dumped in Boston harbor. That would happen in a matter of weeks, cabinet members agreed. Warned by "this searing example," other colonies would quell their pugnacious members, and troubles would end.

"For Relief of the Citizens of Boston"

On March 31, 1774, England's Parliament passed the first of several Coercive Acts that in America came to be called Intolerable Acts. The measure called for the punishment of Massachusetts by prohibiting the loading and unloading of ships in Boston harbor until the East India Company should be paid for tea destroyed in the Boston Tea Party. Value of the tea was arbitrarily set at £15,000.

Enforced by warships of His Majesty the King, the Boston Port Act took effect on June 1. Until then, the busy Massachusetts shipping center had been a beehive of activity with an average of fifty ships arriving and unloading each month. Even before it became operative, it was obvious that the blockade would be virtually 100 percent effective.

Boston could submit—or starve.

News of the Boston Port bill reached the Virginia House of Burgesses in May. Young Thomas Jefferson called for June 1 to be set aside as a day for mourning for "every injury to American rights."

Already, however, other patriots were making plans to help Boston. By the day the port closed, June 1, the first contingent of sheep contributed by Connecticut farmers had reached the city. Rice was sent from the Carolinas—overland for last stages of the journey. Even Quebec responded to the crisis by sending more than 1,000 bushels of wheat. Money plus supplies, needed even more desperately than money, flowed from every English colony in North America.

Denouncing the demand for £15,000 in restitution as "ransom," beleaguered Bostonians subsisted for more than a year largely on food and supplies shipped to them by sympathizers from Georgia to Canada.

More and Better Gunpowder

Antoine Laurent Lavoisier is seldom mentioned in connection with America's War of Independence. He's noted as the founder of modern chemistry and as a victim of the guillotine in 1794.

Yet without the work of Lavoisier, the American Revolution might have taken an entirely different course.

Concerned with the poor quality of gunpowder then manufactured in France, national authorities approached the chemist in the spring of 1774 and presented a challenge to him. Could he—and would he—devote his great knowledge of chemistry to the perfection of powder "warranted to explode when touched by even a few small sparks?"

Lavoisier accepted the challenge and began serious work on gunpowder in August, 1774. It took months of hard work, but he eventually made great improvements in quality. In addition, he drafted plans that would make possible a substantial increase in national production of the vital war material.

It was Lavoisier who served as director of state gunpowder works for the vital period that began in 1776. Because of his achievements, it became possible for France to provide large quantities of good gunpowder to American insurgents.

Scientists remember him for the notable achievement that led to discovery that water is a combination of oxygen and hydrogen; during the turbulent years of the Revolution, frontiersmen who couldn't have pronounced his name used the powder he produced to fight the British.

Tavern Talk

Independence Hall, Old North Church, and a few other buildings in which patriots gathered are famous American landmarks. Not so well known—but almost as important—were the taverns of Colonial America. In and about them much talk and many actions took place.

City Tavern in Philadelphia, built in 1773, boasted that it was fitted "after the latest London mode." But it was to this symbol of England that John Adams repaired when he arrived on August 29, 1774, "dirty, dusty, and fatigued" after answering the call to attend the First Continental Congress. Much of the work of the committees was done in City Tavern, and it was here that informal decisions were made that later reached the floor of the Continental Congress.

Ousted from their formal meeting place in May, 1774, members of Virginia's House of Burgesses adjourned to nearby Raleigh Tavern in Williamsburg. It was here, under leadership of Patrick Henry, that men who had clashed with the royal governor called for "a general congress of the colonies" whose purpose was to consider matters which "the united interests of America may from time to time require."

Patriots who decapitated the famous statue of King George in New York City, July 9, 1776, initially planned to impale the monarch's replica on a pike and erect it in front of the Blue Bell Tavern. British eyewitnesses to the Battle of Lexington swore that the traditional (but not actual) first shot of the Revolution came "from the direction of the Buckman Tavern."

Since taverns were so intimately linked with the beginning and progress of the conflict, it was appropriate that George Washington should take leave from his officers at Fraunces' Tavern in New York City (December 4, 1783). According to Rivington's New York Gazette, "His excellency, having filled a glass of wine, addressed his brave fellow soldiers" packed tightly into the tavern.

Joseph Warren, M.D.

Many early advocates of resistance to English taxes and laws were adventurers who had little or nothing to lose. Some were landed gentry who knew they were risking their fertile acres and spacious mansions. A few were successful professional men who laid their careers on the line in the name of independence.

One such person was Boston physician Joseph Warren. Before matters began to move toward an inevitable conflict, Warren had established "a most handsome practice." He had much to lose and little to gain except satisfaction in doing what he felt to be right.

It was Dr. Warren who presented the famous Suffolk [Mass.] Resolves, adopted at Dedham in Suffolk County in September, 1774. In a sense, the Resolves served as the lighted match that set off the powder keg of rebellion. For the resolutions strongly denounced English policies, urged all citizens to refuse obedience to recent legislation enacted by Parliament, urged nonpayment of taxes, and suggested that militia (largely under local control) should meet weekly for drill.

Taken to the Continental Congress in Philadelphia by Paul Revere, the Suffolk Resolves moved the colonies one step closer to open war.

When war erupted, Dr. Warren was chairman of Boston's Committee of Safety and hence the man responsible for sending Paul Revere on his midnight ride. Warren refused the offer of a commission and insisted on fighting in the ranks like any ordinary enlisted man. During the two-hour engagement at Bunker Hill on June 17, 1775, the fighting physician was killed. The first shaft erected on the site of the present Bunker Hill Monument was a memorial to him.

Myth of the Minutemen

The minutemen of Massachusetts loom large in legends surrounding the Revolution. They are often depicted as crack shots who could pick off redcoats at great distances and as having played a decisive role in the ever-growing conflict. Actually, most minutemen were very poor soldiers who seldom, if ever, became engaged in a real battle. From organization to dissolution the bands made up of these fighting men had a life span of just six months.

On October 14, 1774, the Continental Congress took a bold forward step by adopting a "Declaration of Rights and Grievances." This held that self-government was an inherent right of each British colony—and was an open invitation to armed reprisal.

Massachusetts leaders, nearly always in the forefront of those revolutionary activities, recognized their situation to be particularly precarious. About half of the colony's thirty companies of militia were under the command of staunch Loyalists. The military organization would have to be changed before patriots would have any chance of success.

First through the Worcester Convention, and then in other regional conclaves, patriots succeeded in bringing pressure on Tory colonels. Once resignations of many such officers were secured, the militia was reorganized under new officers—with the express provision that one-third of the men in each company were to be ready to act "at a minute's notice."

A few companies of minutemen were organized in the fall of 1774; others came into existence as late as April, 1775. That month, the colony's Provincial Congress scrapped the minutemen organization in favor of an army of 13,000 volunteers who were urged to enlist for eight months. No patriot played the role of minuteman for more than six months; some had the title for only a few days.

Chessboard Diplomacy

Ardent patriot that he was, Benjamin Franklin preferred to avoid armed conflict between Americans and British. When it was apparent that relationships were becoming strained, the Sage of Philadelphia went to England in order to try to patch up the quarrel. But instead of getting better, the situation rapidly became worse in 1774.

Two brothers, sons of Lord Emanuel Howe, who were destined to play major roles in the ensuing conflict were among the few high-born Englishmen who were eager for peace at practically any price. Vice Admiral Richard, Lord Howe, had distinguished himself in the Seven Years' War and as commander of the Mediterranean Fleet. One of his younger brothers, Major General William Howe, knew he was one of the men in line for possible appointment as commander in chief of land forces in North America.

Both of these distinguished military men had hopes that a special commission could be sent to America to settle differences before any shots were fired. It would be unseemly, however, for either of them to broach such a question in conversation with Benjamin Franklin.

So in the pre-Christmas festivities of 1774, Admiral Howe arranged for his sister-in-law Caroline to meet Franklin at his favorite game: chess. As Franklin himself later reported the encounter, during their second game she expressed hope that "we are not to have a civil war." Franklin indicated his own hope that foes would "kiss and make friends."

As a result of this chessboard diplomacy, Caroline Howe reported to her brother-in-law on Christmas Eve that there was a prospect for peace. That very evening, Lord Howe arranged to be introduced to Franklin. But when word of the informal conversations reached the king, he reacted violently. Appointment of a peace commission was out of the question, he said, because it would make the world think that the "Mother Country is more afraid of continuance of the dispute than the colonies."

Newfoundland Fisheries Placed Off Limits

Early in her expansion as a colonial power, Britain had seen the necessity of regulating fishing in waters she controlled. Several acts dealing with this matter were passed in the eighteenth century. Some of them affected the American colonies—but at worst had only nuisance status.

When Parliament met on November 29, 1774, the tension that was in the air was noticed by most lawmakers present. The official address from the throne took note of the way the Colony of Massachusetts had shown "a most daring spirit of resistance and disobedience to the law." Clearly, drastic measures had to be taken.

Members of the House of Lords and House of Commons showed general concurrence with the king's position by passing a joint resolution stating that "a rebellion at this time actually exists within said Province."

It would be necessary to supplement the armed forces in that region, of course. But many lawmakers agreed that economic measures could bring rebels to heel more swiftly and more easily than military maneuvers.

The lifeblood of Massachusetts—and all New England, for that matter—was the sea. As early as 1641, official statistics noted that 300,000 cod had been exported from the region to the mother country. Each year the importance of the fisheries had mounted. It would choke off the spirit of rebellion in Massachusetts to bar her ships from vital fishing waters off Newfoundland; so felt members of the Lords and Commons.

Against strong opposition by London merchants—who had on their books £2,000,000 pounds in obligations from American merchants—Parliament enacted in December, 1774, a new and much harsher Fishery Act. Vessels from New England colonies were excluded from the Newfoundland fisheries—as well as from trade with Great Britain, Ireland, and the West Indies. Enacted with the hope of quickly restoring order, the severe measure had the opposite effect: embittered seamen heretofore loyal to England hurried to join ranks of rebels.

One Hundred Barrels of Gunpowder

Growing tension between British colonial authorities and American patriots caused men on both sides to place increasing value upon gunpowder. If matters should deteriorate to such a point that either side wished to use force—though the majority of Americans fervently hoped that would never happen—gunpowder could well decide the issue.

Virginia's colonial governor correctly appraised the situation, acted decisively, and seized gunpowder belonging to the colony. Even though he later paid for it, the vital war material remained in his hands.

In New Hampshire—relatively remote from major centers of early strife—Major John Sullivan of the colonial militia wanted to be sure that patriots wouldn't become victims of bullets shot with British powder. So on December 13, 1774, he led a force of about four hundred patriots who attacked Fort William and Mary at New Castle, in Portsmouth Harbor.

Sullivan, other Granite State Volunteers (who carefully donned civilian clothing for the occasion), and civilian patriots captured the commander of the fort. They managed to frighten away the soldiers who should have defended it and triumphantly seized one hundred barrels of gunpowder.

Viewed from any perspective, this was a military operation in spite of the fact that no blood was shed. It took place on December 13, 1774, more than four months before the Battles of Lexington and Concord. Largely overlooked because of attention focused upon battles that followed, the capture of Fort William and Mary for the sake of its store of powder must be considered the beginning of the war if military criteria are used to establish the date on which the Revolution began.

First Five American Generals

Few reference works so much as list the names of the first five American generals: Jedediah Preble, Artemas Ward, Seth Pomeroy, John Thomas, and William Heath.

Massachusetts, hotbed of unrest and hence the target of British reprisals, was ready for armed resistance while most other colonies were still talking of conciliation. Meeting in Charlestown, the Committee of Public Safety took virtually unanimous action in voting to secure "all kinds of warlike stores sufficient for an army of fifteen thousand men." Plans were made for quick mobilization of the militia.

But men and supplies were not enough. Leaders would have to be found—preferably from the ranks of men who had fought for Britain in earlier wars and skirmishes. This was a matter for the Provincial Congress, since it potentially involved the future of the colony.

Meeting in Cambridge, the Congress of the Province of Massachusetts named five "general officers" who were to have supreme command in the event of actual armed warfare. Though their appointment antedated that of any generals who served in the Continental Army, the tenure of most Massachusetts generals was brief, and none distinguished himself against the British.

Small wonder. All of the first five American generals had long been retired from military service; most were past the age for effective duty. Artemas Ward had done well at the Battle of Ticonderoga back in 1758—but was now practically crippled by kidney stones. Seth Pomeroy, first man named and hence having a special niche in history, was almost seventy and had taken off his uniform and donned civilian clothing after the Battle of Louisburg thirty years earlier.

Burke Calls for Conciliation

Though some British leaders considered it imperative to humiliate American colonists who had defied the king's laws, and a few went so far as to wager on a quick end to rebellion once trained soldiers reached Massachusetts in large numbers, one of the strongest voices in Parliament called for conciliation.

Edmund Burke, born in Dublin in 1729, was elected to the British law-making body in 1765 and quickly established a reputation as one of its greatest orators.

From the beginning of the American troubles, Burke called for patience and for mild measures. He opposed the House of Commons bill that ordered the closing of the port of Boston. "The distemper is general," he insisted, "but the punishment is local. Have you considered whether you have troops and ships sufficient to enforce a universal proscription to the trade of the whole continent of America?"

Lawmakers listened, but voted overwhelmingly in favor of the bill. Instead of reducing Burke to silence, official actions seemed to goad him into greater eloquence.

Though not generally familiar to Americans, Burke's speech of March 22, 1775, "On Conciliation with America," was one of the great parliamentary orations of the century. He told fellow lawmakers in stirring sentences that "a fierce spirit of liberty" had grown up in America. It was rooted, he said, in "six capital sources—of descent, of form of government, of religion in the northern provinces, of manners in the southern, of education, of the remoteness of situation from the first mover of government [England's king]."

Burke cited growth of British exports to the New World from £500,000 in 1704 to £5,000,000 in 1772 and called for "trade rather than taxation"—but his oratory fell on deaf ears. Few Americans then knew he defended them.

A New Betting Book

Brooks' Club, a fashionable private club for Britain's men of means and leisure, was long famous for its betting books. Almost any topic of local or national interest could serve as a magnet drawing together men of opposing views—who were eager to risk money upon their ideas.

April, 1775, saw a new betting book opened. Some members of the club felt that the hostilities in the distant North American colonies would prove long and costly. Others were equally sure that untried farmers and frontiersmen could never stand up against an army of His Majesty's trained soldiers.

The first entry recorded in that new betting book read:

"John Burgoyne wagers Charles James Fox one pony [fifty guineas] that he will be home victorious from America by Christmas Day, 1777." To Burgoyne, eighteen months seemed far more than sufficient time to cross the Atlantic, subdue rebellious colonists, and return home in triumph.

Partly as a reward for having drawn up an elaborate (but wholly theoretical) plan "for Conducting the War from the Side of Canada," Burgoyne was given a top post. He reached Boston harbor aboard the *Cerberus* on May 25, about a month after betting fifty guineas on the length of the war.

"Gentleman Johnny," as he liked to be called by his intimates, did participate in some early and spectacular British victories. But just sixty days before he was due to win or lose his bet, he and his entire command laid down their arms at Saratoga, New York. Even so, the Revolution was barely getting under way. Charles Fox collected his wager from the manager of Brooks' Club almost four years before word of British capitulation at Yorktown reached London.

The
Storm Breaks

Mystery of the Shot Heard Round the World

Traditionally, the Battle of Lexington is regarded as the point of no return—the fracas in which first blood was spilled in combat, inevitably leading to a longer and far more costly struggle than either patriots or British expected. Ralph Waldo Emerson's "Hymn Sung at the Completion of the Battle Monument, Concord," on July 4, 1837, credits "embattled farmers" with having fired the first shot—"heard round the world." After two centuries, no one knows who really fired that shot.

In the aftermath of the clash—which by no stretch of the imagination qualifies for the title of "battle"—patriots accused British of pulling the trigger first. Major John Pitcairn was repeatedly accused of having given orders to fire.

There's plenty of reliable evidence that he did use strong language. Preaching on the clash exactly one year after it occurred, the Reverend Jonas Clark of Lexington Church quoted eyewitnesses as saying that Pitcairn (on horseback) approached very close to militiamen and called out: "Ye villains, ye Rebels, disperse! Damn you, disperse!"

Equally reliable witnesses insisted that Pitcairn never gave the order to fire. Many said that the first shot came from behind a stone wall and was aimed at the British; others declared that (without orders) some redcoat with a nervous trigger finger acted without a signal from officers.

There's little chance that the mystery will ever be solved to satisfaction of all historians. So it was an unidentified participant who may have been an embattled farmer or may have been a veteran British trooper who fired the shot whose echo is still reverberating round the world.

"Yankey Scoundrels" Were Poor Shots

In a letter of April 23, 1775, Captain W. G. Evelyn of the famous "King's Own" British regiment described the Battles of Lexington and Concord as "a little fracas that happened here a few days ago between us and the Yankey scoundrels."

The patriots who fought the British that day, Evelyn said, were "the most absolute cowards on the face of the earth, yet they are just now worked up to such a degree of enthusiasm and madness that they are easily persuaded the Lord is to assist them in whatever they undertake.

"The Loss of the rebels cannot be ascertained, but we have reason to think several hundred were killed. Our regiment had four or five men killed, and about twenty-four wounded. Of the whole, about seventy killed, and 150 wounded."

Evelyn's estimate of British casualties was remarkably accurate. As nearly as can be determined, 73 British soldiers died, and 174 were wounded. An additional 26 men were listed as missing in action. That made a total of 273 casualties out of about 1,800 troops.

Minutemen and eager volunteers certainly were not the cowards whom Evelyn described—but neither were they the sharpshooters of American legend. An estimated 3,763 Americans took place in the battle; each man (theoretically, at least) started out with 36 cartridges—or the equivalent in powder and bullets. If each American fired only 18 shots during the day, nearly 75,000 missiles sailed against the enemy.

About one bullet in 300 killed or wounded a British soldier. On an average, only one patriot in fifteen so much as nicked the shoulder of a redcoat—though weapons were often fired at extremely close range.

Israel Bissel, Rider

Longfellow's 1860 poem about "The Midnight Ride of Paul Revere" is one of the most stirring in the English language. Partly because of it, myths cluster around the universally well-known rider like barnacles on an old shrimp boat.

Dr. Joseph Warren, who sent Revere galloping, dispatched three other messengers: William Dawes, Ebenezer Dorr, and Joseph Hall. Aparently on his own initiative Solomon Brown rode all the way to Lexington.

But the really impressive ride linked with events of April 19, 1775, was a five-day feat by a man whose name dropped out of history. Iz Bissel was a veteran postrider on the Boston to New York run. He was an ordinary working man set apart from the company that included Paul Revere by the rigid social distinctions of colonial America.

Bissel got his orders from Colonel Joseph Palmer of Braintree, Massachusetts. Palmer received sketchy word about the Battle of Lexington and wrote out a message to which he put his signature in case it should be challenged.

"The bearer Israel Bissel is charged to alarm the Country quite to Connecticut," Palmer wrote. "All persons are desired to furnish him with fresh horses, as they may be needed."

Riding hell-for-leather, Iz Bissel covered the roller coaster road to Worcester, Massachusetts, in just two hours. Tradition says his horse died under him at the site of present-day Worcester city hall. He got a new one and kept going. By April 21 he was in New Haven—and on Manhattan Island two days later. He shouted word of Lexington to crowds of church goers, then climbed back on his horse and raced through New Jersey. He didn't stop until he reached Philadelphia on April 25, 118 hours from his starting point at Watertown, Massachusetts, setting a record as a long-distance courier.

Olive Branch Rejected

In the aftermath of Lexington, Concord, and Breed's Hill it was clear that colonists would have to risk everything by a fight to the end—or gain time and save something by a compromise with Britain.

Colonial leaders prepared a placative—almost obsequious—petition beseeching England's king "to procure us relief from our afflicting fears and jealousies . . . and to settle peace through every part of our Dominions."

Addressed to "Most Gracious Sovereign" by men who styled themselves "your Majesty's faithful subjects," the message was signed by all members of the Continental Congress except George Washington and a few others who were absent on military duties.

John Adams immediately labelled the document the "Olive Branch"—a name that has stuck to it ever since. Adams and other key leaders regarded the petition as a calculated risk. If acted upon by George III it would take much of the steam out of the revoluntionary movement. But if pushed aside or rejected outright, it would convert many loyalists into patriots.

William Penn's grandson, Richard, was chosen as bearer of the message. He went to England (1775) on a fast packet, dutifully requested the gracious leave of King George to present him with a "most urgent message from his dutiful subjects in the North American colonies."

George III—who had already determined upon a course that left no room for compromise—flatly refused to receive Penn or even to read the petition that he brought with him. When word reached America that the Olive Branch had been refused, many leaders who had wavered in their views threw their weight on the side of armed resistance—and the way was paved for adoption of the Declaration of Independence.

Gage's Proclamation Penned by Playwright

General Thomas Gage, Governor of Massachusetts, was fully aware that matters had deteriorated badly by the spring of 1775. He consulted fellow officials and decided to handle the delicate situation by issuing an official proclamation.

Gage was a man of action, uncomfortable with pen and paper. So he turned to a colleague with considerable experience as a playwright. Once the playwright-turned-soldier had penned the terms he felt suitable, Gage made few changes in it. Though issued over his own signature, it was quickly recognized in England as having come from another man's hand.

Few official statements intended to put a stop to troublemakers have ever been so badly phrased.

"Whereas, the infatuated multitude, who have long suffered themselves to be conducted by certain well known incendiaries and traitors, in a fatal progression of crimes against the constitutional authority of the State, have at length proceeded to avowed Rebellion," began the famous document of June 12, 1775, "it only remains for those who are invested with supreme rule . . . to prove they do not bear the sword in vain."

In Governor Gage's name, the proclamation insisted that he was making "the last effort within the bounds of my duty to spare the effusion of blood." So in the name of the King of England, he offered "his most gracious pardon" to all persons who would lay down their arms—except for Samuel Adams and John Hancock. Martial law was proclaimed throughout the province. Instead of soothing angry colonists, this proclamation spurred rebels to dig in at Breed's Hill and Bunker Hill—and begin to fight in earnest.

Today it is universally recognized among scholars that "Gentleman Johnny" Burgoyne, playwright, wrote the proclamation that led to the Battle of Bunker Hill.

First Naval Battle

Like a number of land engagements in which casualties were out of all proportion to psychological impact, the first naval battle didn't seriously hamper British activities. It merely fanned the fires of patriotism by showing that Americans actually could defeat professionals from across the Atlantic.

News of the Battles of Lexington and Concord—themselves of little military significance—reached the village of Machias, Maine, some time late in the week of June 4, 1775. On Sunday the eleventh, while crewmen of H.M.S. *Margaretta* were attending church services with their commanding officer, patriots slipped into the harbor and took over two commercial vessels.

The sloops *Polly* and *Unity* lay at anchor, waiting for cargoes of lumber consigned to British forces occupying Boston. Midshipman James Moore, commander of the *Margaretta*, concluded that discretion was the better part of valor. Though his own vessel had four light cannons and the patriots had only a few muskets plus axes and pitchforks, he decided to flee.

Chasing the British ship in the *Unity*, patriots elected Jeremiah O'Brien as captain. They outsailed the British vessel and after hand to hand fighting took the *Margaretta* as America's first naval prize of the war.

Renamed the *Machias Liberty*, the onetime sloop *Unity* saw heavy fighting two weeks later off the coast of Maine, where the British schooner *Diligent* and her tender were captured. Rejoining the captured *Polly*, O'Brien's vessel became flagship of the first naval squadron of Massachusetts' colonial navy.

Assault at High Tide

American-born General Sir Henry Clinton was confident that rebel forces concentrated in Boston would be defeated easily and quickly. Rebels had no heavy cannon. Clinton's fleet included five medium-sized warships: H.M.S. *Lively*, *Falcon*, *Cerebus*, *Glasgow*, and *Symmetry*.

But the British trump card in the clash that Clinton was sure would be little more than a skirmish was the huge H.M.S. *Somerset*—armed with three tiers of big guns. Any amateur could see that the rebels could be blasted off the top side of the earth in minutes.

There was just one difficulty. Clinton couldn't risk running the *Somerset* and other vessels aground. The big warship drew so much water that attack would have to be launched precisely at high tide.

Writing in his journal on the evening of June 6, the British commander noted the cost of this factor. "If we were of active disposition," he recorded, "we should be landed tomorrow at daybreak. As it is, I fear it must be postponed until two." Experts had assured him that high tide would come precisely at that hour.

With the decision concerning time of attack made, Clinton retired for the night. Next day the attack was launched to coincide with high tide. But the delay had permitted patriots to throw up earthworks on Breed's Hill—so that though British forces did take it and Bunker Hill, it was at enormous cost through loss of about one thousand men.

It took Britain many months to field replacements for those 1,000 men—months during which time Colonial forces gained both strength and skill. Time bought by the fact that high tide came at two o'clock in the afternoon instead of at dawn on June 17, 1775, helped prevent Britain from quickly crushing what at first was regarded as an impertinent uprising of farmers and merchants.

In Quest of a Name

A majority of influential leaders in most major English colonies (but never all leaders in all colonies) found it comparatively easy in the heated atmosphere of 1775 to agree that separation from the mother country was not merely desirable but essential. To reach this point of view was much easier than to devise a suitable name for the new nation that was in the process of being formed.

Numerous documents and proclamations settled for "United Colonies." Others specified "all the English colonies on this continent." Yet the most frequent of all early usages was "The United Colonies of North America." Printed rules for troops, issued on June 30, 1775, specified the parent body to whom troops were responsible as being "The Twelve United English Colonies of North-America."

But the term "colony" didn't seem exactly appropriate for sovereign political entities. By June, 1776, "state" had come into such wide usage that the Virginia delegation proposed to the Continental Congress that these "United Colonies are, and of right out to be, free and independent States."

This emphasis made it easy for Thomas Jefferson to adopt bold new terminology in framing the Declaration of Independence. That document dubbed the still-unformed nation as "The United States of America."

From the Declaration of Independence, that label passed into the 1777 Articles of Confederation and eventually into the Constitution that was adopted in 1787. Long before that, though, the name was firmly fixed. Washington's commission (June 17, 1775) and his instructions from Congress, issued three days later, placed him at the head of the armed forces of the United States of America.

Fifty Acres and Five Dollars

Arrival in Boston of General Sir William Howe, May, 1775, changed the climate of the struggle between colonists and British administrators. Howe, in contrast with many British leaders, took a hard line and stuck to it. "Rebels must be dealt with roughly," he noted in an official report. As a professional soldier, he had no doubt of his ability to deal very roughly, indeed.

Partly to augment his armed forces, partly in an attempt to sow dissension among colonists, Howe engaged in a special recruitment program, Beginning in July, 1775, he offered what for the time seemed an immense bounty to any man who would desert the cause of the Continentals and don the uniform of a British soldier.

A broadside issued on behalf of the First Battalion of Pennsylvania Loyalists was typical of Howe's efforts. It appealed to "ALL INTREPID ABLE-bodied HEROES who are willing to serve His Majesty King George the Third, in defence of Their Country, Laws and Constitution, against the arbitrary Usurpations of a tyrannical Congress." Recruits, Howe promised, "have now not only an Opportunity of manifesting their Spirit, by assisting in reducing to Obedience their too-long deluded Countrymen, but also of acquiring the polite Accomplishments of a Soldier, by serving only two Years, or during the present Rebellion in America."

Though Howe was inordinately confident that the rebellion wouldn't last two years, he offered "spirited Fellows" who enlisted in his forces a bounty "at the End of the War, besides their Laurels, 50 Acres of Land, where every gallant Hero may retire" in addition to "FIVE DOLLARS, besides Arms, Cloathing and Accoutrements" issued upon actual enlistment. Hundreds took the bait, and each got his $5 enlistment fee—but no loyalist of American birth was ever paid off on the promise of fifty acres for retirement.

A Captured Letter Fans the Fire

Benjamin Hichborn, a young Boston lawyer who had a nodding acquaintance with John Adams, approached the ardent patriot for a personal favor in the summer of 1775. As Adams' own papers recount the event, Hichborn wanted to serve as a courier for the older man.

"He prayed I would write if it were only a Line to my Family, for he said, as he had served his Clerkship with Mr. Fitch he was suspected and represented as a Tory, and this Reputation would be his ruin, if it could not be corrected, for nobody would employ him at the Bar."

Adams, then in Philadelphia, first refused the request. Then "To get rid of his importunity, I took my Penn, and wrote a very few Lines to my Wife and about an equal Number to General James Warren."

Clutching the letters, Hichborn set out to deliver them—and prove his loyalty to the cause of the challengers of English rule. He made it as far as Conanicut Ferry, Narragansett Bay. Captured by the British he made a clumsy attempt to destroy the letters but didn't succeed.

Adams' captured letter to General Warren was published on August 17 in the *Massachusetts Gazette and Boston Weekly News Letter,* then widely reprinted. The original was forwarded by Vice Admiral Samuel Graves to the Admiralty Office in London.

According to printed version, Adams wanted the Continental Congress to establish a government for all of North America. He was eager to frame a constitution, to establish a navy, and to open American ports to all ships except those from England.

The captured letter created a furor in England and helped to fan the fires of revolution in America. Adams always insisted that the British tampered with his language before publishing it—but since the original has never been found, there is no way to know whether he was actively agitating in favor of revolution almost a year before the Declaration of Independence was framed.

War Profiteers Sold Men to British

Once unequivocal decisions were reached and legislation was enacted to support those decisions, King George III had to have armed men to enforce edicts. Britain herself had a small standing army—not nearly large enough to provide the troops needed in North America. In spite of recruitment methods of doubtful legal standing, it was clear that it would be impossible to get enough English soldiers.

Envoys approached Catherine the Great of Russia (whom the English monarch affectionately addressed as "Sister Kitty"), but were quickly rebuffed. Holland had plenty of well-trained men, but refused to make them available.

In this critical situation the English monarch of German descent turned to the princes of Germany. These monarchs ruled with absolute power, but had relatively few subjects living in small regions. Most already had iron-clad systems of recruitment for military service plus access to good schools for training men in combat.

George III dangled the most enticing bait of all—gold. In return for each soldier furnished, the prince of that soldier's realm received more than £7 in cash in "levy money." A similar payment was stipulated in return for every man killed—with three men wounded to count as one dead. During a visit to London in September, 1775, the prince of Hesse-Cassel accepted the gracious terms of his "cousin," and other German rulers soon did the same.

Hesse-Cassel originally contracted to provide 12,000 men and eventually sent more. Others came from Brunswick, Hesse-Hanau, Anspach-Bayreuth, Waldeck, and Anhalt-Zerbst. The total number of troops ostensibly "rented," but for practical purposes actually sold, exceeded 30,000. Of these an estimated 12,000 never returned home. Hesse-Cassel alone, one of the least important principalities in Europe, realized a profit of more than $5,000,000 from men rented to the British to fight the Americans.

Benedict Arnold's Impossible March

During the summer of 1775, thirty-four-year-old Colonel Benedict Arnold went to Cambridge, Massachusetts, and laid before George Washington a novel plan. Send two colonial forces into Canada, he urged, and capture Quebec—key to the whole vast region. One force could go by way of lakes George and Champlain and the Richelieu River. The other—which Arnold himself offered to lead—would take a dangerous and little-known passage by way of the Kennebec and Chaudiere rivers.

Washington approved the undertaking. Hence the man who later became infamous as a traitor to his country headed an expedition that made Washington's crossing of the Delaware seem like child's play and was comparable with Valley Forge in terms of hardship.

Benedict Arnold and his contingent left Cambridge on September 13, 1775. At Newburyport, Massachusetts, they took to the sea briefly, landing at the mouth of the Kennebec river where two hundred bateaux were supposed to be waiting. One glance showed that the boats had been built from green lumber and were not suited for the dangerous expedition, but Arnold ordered his men to move forward.

By mid-October everything edible—even candles—had been consumed, and troops were forced to live off the land. Private George Morison of the Pennsylvania Rifles described the way he and his comrades waded through icy mire, often falling and never getting up again. Writing to General Richard Montgomery, Arnold himself said, "We have hauled our bateaux over falls, up rapid streams and marched through morasses, thick woods, and over mountains about 320 miles."

The impossible march took remnants of Arnold's command to the St. Lawrence river on November 8. Joined by General Montgomery and his forces, Americans attacked Quebec on December 31—only to suffer a disastrous defeat.

Chief Physician to the American Army

Benjamin Church, M.D., had studied in London and had built up a handsome practice before tensions between Britain and her American colonies reached the crisis point. On the outbreak of hostilities, Church immediately offered his services and was placed in charge of medical affairs for the Continental army outside Boston. Though he never had the title, for practical purposes he was the first Surgeon General of the U. S. Army.

James Warren of Massachusetts, paymaster general of the Continental Army for a year and member of the navy board for the eastern department until 1781, sent a hasty letter to John Adams on October 1, 1775. Writing from Watertown, near Boston, he explained to the future President that "an event has lately taken place here which makes much noise, and gives me much uneasiness. Dr. Church has been detected in a correspondence with the enemy, at least so far that a letter wrote by him in a curious cypher and directed to Major Cane (who is an officer in the Royal army and one of Gage's family) has been intercepted."

Correspondence, said Warren, was forwarded by means of "an infamous hussy" with whom "the Doctor has formed an infamous connection."

George Washington himself presided over the court-martial of Benjamin Church. Evidence presented was ambiguous and wouldn't stand up in present-day U. S. courts. Still, the commander in chief pressed for conviction. As a result the physician was imprisoned for a time; after he was paroled, he sailed for the West Indies and was lost at sea. Many patriots as well as loyalists lauded him as a martyr given an unjust sentence.

In 1930, papers of British General Thomas Gage were brought to the University of Michigan—and found to include numerous traitorous letters from Church giving the British leader detailed information and prodding him into the decision that led to the Battle of Concord, April 19, 1775.

Benjamin Thompson, Count Rumford

Born in Woburn, Massachusetts, in 1753, Benjamin Thompson was one of the few natives of North America to enter the ranks of European nobility. Though he was an avowed loyalist, he might have stayed in America had he not been accused by patriots of spying for the British. Though no proof of covert activities was produced then or later, he was handled so roughly by his countrymen that on October 13, 1775, he left his native country aboard the British frigate *Scarborough.*

English scientists and scholars welcomed Thompson with open arms; he had already begun to make a reputation as an original investigator. Elected to membership in the Royal Society, he entered the military service and for a few months in 1782-83 fought against his own countrymen.

Once hostilities ended, Benjamin Thompson retired from active military service on half pay—as a colonel of the King's Dragoons.Touring the continent, he met and impressed the field marshal of France—who gave him a letter of introduction to the Elector of Bavaria. With the permission of England's king, Thompson—already having been made a knight by that monarch—entered the service of Bavaria. He so distinguished himself that the Elector made the native of America a nobleman of the Holy Roman Empire under the title of Count Rumford.

President John Adams, as a gesture of restitution for the expatriate, offered him the choice of two posts: lieutenant and inspector of artillery in the U. S. Army or superintendent of the military academy at West Point. Rumford declined both places, but in his will the man who fled under accusations of spying left funds to endow a professorship of physics at Harvard University.

Silliest Contest in History

Americans who were busy digging in for a long struggle with Britain got little news about activities of their supporters in the mother country. One of them Charles James Fox, gained lasting fame as an orator because of speeches made opposing the official policies for dealing with "the troubles in North America." A Tory, Fox served in the Cabinet as a lord of admiralty and of treasury before he became an outspoken opponent of his king's way of handling problems with colonists.

Until early 1774, Fox was chiefly noted as a gambler who often spent the entire night at Almack's Club. His losses were so great that it cost his father £140,000 to settle his debts during the winter of 1773-74.

On March 24, he made his debut as a legislative orator by arguing that parliament—not the king—must deal with America. He spoke in favor of repeal of the tea duty and on April 19 voted for repeal. For the next two or three years, whenever any matter affecting North America was discussed in Parliament, Fox could be depended upon to deliver an oration—usually pungent and moving, always favoring colonists against king, and practically always futile.

Many of his admirers declared that Fox delivered the most moving oration of his career when parliament convened on October 26, 1775. It was the first official conclave since word of the Battle of Concord had reached London—and anti-American leaders were angry. With England's Prime Minister sitting in the audience of lawmakers, Fox said:

"I cannot consent to the bloody consequences of so silly a contest about so silly an object, conducted in the silliest manner that history has ever furnished an instance of." The Prime Minister, said Fox, had lost more than Alexander the Great ever gained: a whole continent. Though hopelessly outnumbered when votes were cast, the highborn gambler continued to speak so eloquently in defense of America that he is now remembered as one of England's greatest orators.

Esek Hopkins, Commander in Chief

Many key leaders of the Continental Congress felt that the new nation needed a navy as badly as an army. Official action leading to establishment of the Continental Navy began in October, 1775, and moved swiftly. Within thirty days, four vessels were purchased: the *Alfred, Columbus, Andrew Doria,* and *Cabot.*

Before these merchant ships that had been transformed into fighting craft could function, the navy had to have a head. Congress looked the country over, picked a man with long and wide experience.

Born near North Scituate, Rhode Island, on April 26, 1718, Esek Hopkins went to sea at age twenty. Eventually he became owner of a fleet of merchant vessels. Based on his experience with them, he was a successful privateer during the Seven Years' War (1756-63).

Hopkins was named commander in chief of the Continental Navy on November 5, 1775. He didn't actually assume his duties until December 22, by which time formal regulations for the navy (based almost entirely on British precedents) had been adopted and eighteen junior officers had been named. Hopkins boarded the *Alfred* on December 22 with a young lieutenant named John Paul Jones.

Naval operations were hampered by congressional delays plus insistence that lawmakers, not sailors, should make battle plans. Hopkins unsuccessfully tried to carry out orders, lost many of his men because of illness, and was suspended from command on March 26, 1777. There was nearly a year of delay—until January 2, 1778—before he was formally dismissed from service.

His vacant post was not filled. The infant Continental Navy, unlike the Army, disintegrated. Individual commanders —notably John Paul Jones—and privateers fought most naval engagements of the war, and it was not until peace came that the Navy became a formidable fighting force.

British Daring Leads to Victory

General Sir Guy Carleton, Governor of Canada, sensed that the province was the target of American plans when a poorly organized attack was made upon Montreal on September 25, 1775. This assault had no important result except the capture of Ethan Allen by the British.

But when St. Johns on the Richelieu fell to Continental forces on November 2, the royal governor knew that the fate of Canada—and perhaps of the entire British establishment in North America—hung in the balance. With eleven ships loaded chiefly with ammunition, Carleton managed to get into the St. Lawrence River and make his escape from Montreal before the city was captured on November 13.

Clearly, the Continentals could have only one major Canadian objective left: Quebec. It was imperative that the governor himself reach the outpost city. But rebel guns commanded the long narrows at Sorel, which seemed to make westward passage by water impossible to the British.

In one of the most daring operations of the entire conflict, the royal governor of Canada disguised himself as a peasant and —without troops to guard him—climbed into a whaling ship. Captain Bouchette, nicknamed *La Tourte* ("the pigeon") because of his reputation for fast sailing, assured him that it was, indeed, possible to slip past rebel guns.

Risking his life every instant, Carleton went through nine miles of narrows, then reached open water and found a British armed brig that took him on to Quebec. Once there he proclaimed martial law and gave male citizens the option of enlisting in the militia or leaving the town. Quick and decisive action at Quebec on the heels of a danger-filled journey, led to overwhelming victory by the British—and prevented seizure of Canada by Benedict Arnold as a base from which to move against redcoats in colonies to the south.

First Valuable Prize

Acting in his role of commander in chief of the army, George Washington recognized the urgency of attacking British shipping. His small fleet fitted out in the fall of 1775 was manned by a motley group of sailors and officers. One of them, John Manley, was given a commission as a captain in the army before he was assigned to command the schooner *Lee*.

In one of the few naval engagements of modern time which involved an army officer as a ship's captain, Manley attacked and captured the British brigantine *Nancy*.

The vessel itself was of little importance. But its cargo constituted the first valuable prize of the war. After November, 1775, capture of the ship, patriots made a careful inventory; to their amazed delight they were able to report to Washington that the *Nancy* had yielded:

> 2,000 muskets
> 100,000 flints
> 30,000 round shot
> 30 tons of musket shot
> 1 brass mortar

Though the mortar wasn't a huge one even by contemporary standards (13 inches), it represented a tremendous psychological triumph. Now the British would feel the effect of one of their own big guns!

At Manley's suggestion, the three-thousand-pound weapon was dubbed "Congress" in a formal christening ceremony—then put into service against its makers.

Durham's Boats

Had it not been for a tangled chain of circumstances, George Washington couldn't even have attempted to cross the Delaware River in order to attack British forces in Trenton, New Jersey. He assembled about 2,400 men under his own command on Christmas Day, 1775, and prepared to embark because he had assembled a flotilla of Durham boats.

Named for Robert Durham, who first began making them about 1750, the boats were peculiar to the Delaware. Great numbers of them plied its waters, but no boats of similar design were to be found anywhere else in North America.

Discovery of iron ore in Bucks County about the turn of the century had led to erection of the Durham Iron Works in 1727. There was plenty of good ore—but it went begging because of difficulties involved in getting it to market. That's why Robert Durham designed and began building big black boats ranging from forty to sixty feet in length and designed to transport great quantities of iron ore to Philadelphia.

Most boats were about eight feet wide; all were pointed at both ends so that they could move in either direction. In spite of their size, Durham boats drew less than twenty inches of water.

Had an expert in logistics set out to design a boat capable of transporting up to fifteen tons of men, horses, and artillery, he couldn't have improved on the Durham boat. Availability of these special craft affected the course of history, for without them Washington's famous crossing of the Delaware would have been utterly impossible.

First Official Flag Was Ambiguous

Since it was to be about eighteen months before Congress adopted the Stars and Stripes to symbolize the unity of the nation in process of being formed, it seemed logical that Continental forces should have their own special battle emblem.

The flag adopted as a result of this need is known as the Grand Union or Great Union. Out of respect to the British crown, the familiar Jack (cross-like emblem for which the British Jack was named) had a prominent place in the upper corner of the flag designed by defiant colonists.

To symbolize unity of the colonies, America's first official flag had thirteen red and white stripes. Rebels and Tories alike realized that the unity was more symbolic than real; each colony still retained its identity and independence, and at the national level there was little real power.

It was the Grand Union flag George Washington first raised in battle on the first day of 1776. Laying siege to British-held Boston, the commander in chief ordered that the new standard should be hoisted to the top of a salvaged ship's mast, more than seventy feet tall. There was no way that British defenders of the port could fail to see it.

They saw it and mistakenly took it to be a signal of submission, since it included in the upper left corner (or canton) the long-familiar Jack of the British flag. Even though the new national emblem was found to be ambiguous from the start, it took about a year and one-half to develop "Old Glory," with stars replacing the British Jack.

Forty-seven Pages of Common Sense

Authors abounded on both sides of the British-American conflict. Books in defense of the crown and the policies of the king poured from printing presses on both sides of the Atlantic, along with a much smaller number of volumes that openly advocated resistance by all possible means.

One of the most influential of the Revolutionary books was also one of the smallest. Thomas Paine, born and reared in England, tried his hand at a variety of trades. He was successively a corset maker, collector of excise taxes, schoolteacher, tobacconist, and grocer. He showed a truly amazing ability to fail at practically everything he did.

But with the mounting climate of tension producing polarization both in Britain and in America, the man who failed at everything he tried became a pamphleteer. R. Bell, of Third Street in Philadelphia, took a financial risk when he agreed to issue a forty-seven page book by Paine in January, 1776. Called *Common Sense,* it appealed not to the common sense of the colonists, but to their emotions.

"Now is the seed-time of continental union, faith and honor," Paine declared. "Time hath found us. Time hath found us!" As though his theme needed any additional amplification, he concluded his little book with a single boldface line that read: **"The Free and Independent States of America."**

Short as it was, *Common Sense* served its purpose well. Men who read and pondered its inflammatory message seldom continued to try to straddle the fence. Some, according to the *Annual Register,* became loyalists though they had been "among the most forward in opposing the claims of the crown and parliament." For each loyalist that *Common Sense* made, a dozen ardent patriots were created. No other short book published during the eighteenth century had so profound an influence upon the course of world history.

One Thousand Lashes

British discipline, always harsh, became increasingly severe as commanders found it difficult to prevent their men from plundering the civilian countryside. Long-standing regulations made the death penalty a last resort, usually reserved for battlefield deserters and for traitors. But there was a penalty just short of death that could be used at the discretion of any general officer.

General Sir William Howe turned to the use of that penalty as early as January, 1776. Reporting to London, he said that "robberies and housebreaking have got to such a height that some examples have to be made."

That month, a court-martial condemned seven enlisted men to severe floggings; several got the maximum: 1,000 lashes.

A soldier who was punished by flogging was tied to a post formed by crossed halberds. Drummers administered the cat-o'nine-tails. Each man gave twenty-five lashes, then passed the whip along to a comrade. Experience had indicated that 1,000 lashes in a single session usually led to death, so men who received the maximum sentence of flogging could expect four weekly periods of punishment of 250 lashes. At the end of each period, buckets of salt water were poured over cut and bleeding backs.

Women who accompanied the troops were theoretically subject to the same discipline as their husbands or lovers. There is no record that a female camp follower ever received 1,000 lashes, but Howe's officers sentenced Isabella McMahon to 100 lashes "on the bare back at the cart's tail," and the sentence was carried out by drummers.

Severity of punishment for looting and pillaging showed no direct correlation with the number of offenses committed; even when threatened with 1,000 lashes many a redcoat couldn't resist an opportunity to seize civilian property.

Virginia's Fighting Parson

Peter Mühlenberg won the hearts of the people of Woodstock, Virginia, soon after he became pastor of the town's German Lutheran church late in 1772. Earlier he had served Lutheran churches along the Delaware River—and had gone to London to be ordained as a priest of the Church of England.

In spite of Anglican ties, he was an outspoken advocate of independence and became a community leader in the cause. No one was greatly surprised when he became chairman of the Committee on Public Safety for Dunmore County.

But in January, 1776, he created an uproar in the community. Many visitors crowded the church to hear what had been billed as his farewell sermon—though only his most intimate friends knew what he intended to do. Mühlenberg preached on the text: "To every thing there is a season, and a time to every purpose under the heaven" (Eccles. 3:1).

At the conclusion of his sermon the priest threw off his clerical gown and stood before the members of the parish in the uniform of a militia officer. Germans from the Shenandoah Valley flocked to join the 8th Virginia Regiment when it was known that he would serve as its commander. Mühlenberg fought at Sullivan's Island in June, 1776, and won his commission as brigadier general in the Continental Army the following February. He was with Washington at Valley Forge and served for a time as second in command under von Steuben.

On September 30, 1783, he was made major general, the highest rank of any clergyman on either side in the conflict.

The Guns of Ticonderoga

Early in 1775 Continental leaders recognized British-held Fort Ticonderoga to be a prize worth seeking. The isolated and dilapidated old fortress had little strategic value—but it was known to be equipped with many fine European-made cannon, of which Washington and his forces were woefully short.

An expedition was organized, but bickering among leaders delayed action. With Ethan Allen of Vermont as senior leader, an American task force subdued the garrison of forty-three men in May, 1775. But no one made a move to put the precious artillery pieces into action.

Months later, Boston-born Colonel Henry Knox, age twenty-four, personally proposed a plan to Washington. With the approval of the commander in chief, Knox and his brother William led a small force to the distant fortress. They reached Ticonderoga on December 5, 1775, and when they took inventory they found themselves confronted by 119,900 pounds of iron: fourteen mortars and coehorns, two howitzers, and forty-three cannon —the most important but also the heaviest pieces of all.

Knox floated the weapons to Fort George at the southern end of Lake George. With winter snow already thick on the ground, he built sleds and bought all the oxen and horses in the region. Against enormous obstacles—Knox later said he did not take off his clothes day or night for forty days—the vanguard of the artillery train reached Cambridge on January 24, 1776.

Hastily put in place as a result of daring and ingenuity by one-time bookseller Knox, the guns of Ticonderoga tipped the scales in favor of rebel forces and compelled British forces under Howe to evacuate Boston.

King George and the Broadswords

Except as ornaments, swords played an insignificant role in the Revolution. These weapons—whether narrow or broad—had been made obsolete generations earlier. But Scotsmen who had fought with the Stuarts against King George II of England in 1745 habitually referred to their own fighting men as "Broadswords."

The outbreak of hostilities in the New World caused a strange shift of loyalty on the part of many Scots. Great numbers of them were concentrated in the Carolinas. Instead of maintaining their inherited opposition to the British crown, they became ardent loyalists and set out to help subdue rebels.

Donald McDonald recruited a band that at its peak numbered nearly 1,500 men—McDonalds, McKenzies, MacLeods, Camerons, and other Scots. They took orders from the Tory governor of North Carolina, who (like the governor of Virginia) had taken refuge aboard a British warship that was used as a base of operations.

Shouting their battle cry of "King George and the Broadswords!" the Scots were fearful opponents. For two months they made successful forays up and down the coast of North Carolina. Then they met a numerically smaller band of patriots led by Colonel Richard Caswell and Colonel John Alexander Lillington. The chief clash came at Moore's Creek Bridge on February 27, 1776.

More than 850 clansmen (who had for reasons still not quite clear switched loyalty and gone over to the support of the king they themselves had once hated) became prisoners of the smaller patriot force. This was the largest band of prisoners yet captured by American insurgents—and one of the largest in early years of the war.

The Rescue of Major John Small

Like great numbers of other British officers, Major John Small had spent years of his military career in North America. During the British attempt to hold Boston in the winter of 1775-76, the veteran of the French and Indian Wars must have known that capitulation was inevitable.

There were seven thousand or more redcoats, but Washington led more than twice as many men. True, an estimated two thousand of Washington's soldiers didn't even have muskets, but sooner or later the sheer weight of numbers would lead to British collapse.

Henry Knox hastened the coming of that collapse by successfully bringing to Boston a quantity of artillery pieces he had seized at Ft. Ticonderoga. Without reaching a formal agreement, both Washington and Howe by their actions signaled to one another that they would not destroy the city. The cannon brought by Knox meant, however, that the end was near for British forces of occupation.

During one of the final skirmishes before Howe pulled out on St. Patrick's Day, advancing British grenadiers found themselves under merciless fire from patriots. Many enlisted men threw down their weapons and ran for their lives.

Major John Small, who had been leading a detachment, refused to run. As a result he found himself suddenly alone —deserted by his own men. Three or four Continental soldiers, clustered together on a slight incline just ahead of him, raised their muskets simultaneously and aimed at him. At that instant, General Israel Putnam of the Continental Army dashed up on his horse and with his sword knocked up the guns in order to save the life of John Small—with whom he had fought in the French and Indian War.

Pierre Augustin Caron de Beaumarchais

Those Americans who remember Beaumarchais at all are likely to think of him as the author of "The Barber of Seville" (first performed in 1775) and "The Marriage of Figaro" (first performed in 1784). Actually, the playwright-speculator-patriot played a major role in American independence.

Beaumarchais first became acquainted with American patriots in 1775 when he was in London on a mission for his king. Instantly he sensed an opportunity to boost the fortunes of France by helping to humiliate and weaken England. A full year before the Declaration of Independence was adopted, the French playwright was in Flanders buying arms and establishing a base from which to smuggle them to North America.

With all the skill that he poured into his immortal plays, he wrote letter after letter to King Louis XVI. All of them emphasized one theme: with quick but secret aid from France, the Americans would be victorious in their struggle against Britain. This would have the effect of both reducing the power of Britain and raising the prestige of France.

For Beaumarchais, the grandest day of his life was May 2, 1776. King Louis XVI that day signed documents that committed France to aiding the American rebels—in violation of Anglo-French treaties.

In order to keep the matter secret, Beaumarchais set up and operated the firm of Hortalez & Co. Initially financed by a contribution of one million livres from Louis XVI, it eventually spent more than forty million livres for arms and supplies—most of the money never being repaid.

Beaumarchais used the *Amphitrite* and the *Mercure* to send cannon, small arms, blankets, clothing, and gunpowder to the New World in time to help the foes of Britain win the day at Saratoga—the battle seen by many later analysts as the turning point of the Revolution.

Silas Deane's Sympathetic Ink

Emphasis upon Benjamin Franklin's role in dealing with French leaders has overshadowed the man who both went there earlier and outranked the exprinter. Silas Deane, a member of the Committee of Secret Correspondence that was organized on November 29, 1775, left Philadelphia the following March with two commissions. Both were top secret.

The first came from a commercial committee of the Continental Congress. Under it, Deane was authorized to secure products of the colonies and to ship them abroad in order to get money with which to buy supplies needed in the New World.

Instructions of the Committee of Secret Correspondence put Deane in charge of buying clothing and arms for at least 25,000 men—along with munitions and artillery. He was to use credit where he could and to pay cash where required.

Deane arrived in France on May 4, 1776, and on that day wrote a seemingly innocent personal letter. Between the lines of it, however, he inserted a brief message written in "sympathetic" or invisible ink. There is no record of earlier U. S. diplomatic correspondence employing tools of the spy.

He remained in France for two years, carrying on a voluminous correspondence—much of which was lost because ships bearing letters were captured by the British. Surviving specimens indicate, though, that Deane relied heavily on a tried and tested mixture of cobalt chloride, glycerin, and water. This fluid produces writing that disappears when dry—but becomes visible when held over heat. Many messages transmitted by means of invisible ink dealt with commercial affairs, but one of them gave Congress the first authentic news of British determination to use military power to crush the spirit of resistance among patriots.

Edward Bancroft, Double Agent

Born in Massachusetts in 1744, Edward Bancroft was educated as a physician in England, but never entered active medical practice. In June, 1776, at age thirty-two he found something a great deal better—a highly lucrative post as double agent for the British Secret Service.

Though not nearly so well known as Benedict Arnold, Bancroft is now recognized as having done much more harm to the cause of American patriots than did the general who sold out to the British.

Details about Bancroft and his mission weren't known until 1889, when scholar B. F. Stevens published facsimilies of British Secret Service reports compiled during the Revolution.

Bancroft formed a close friendship with Benjamin Franklin and Silas Deane. To them he posed as a part-time spy bringing them news about British military and naval plans every time he returned to Paris from one of his frequent visits to London.

Actually, the American-born Fellow (or member) of England's noted Royal Society was feeding information to the British on a schedule. Papers made public nearly a century after his death revealed that every Tuesday evening at 9:30, a messenger came to "the tree pointed at the south terrace of the Tuileries" and extracted from a hole in its root a bottle containing one of Bancroft's communiqués.

His reports were so complete and timely that for nearly a year (May, 1777, to April, 1778) the Continental Congress didn't receive a line from its representatives in France. Every ship carrying a message was intercepted and captured, thanks to Bancroft. When the Treaty of 1778 was signed, Bancroft had a copy of it in London within forty-eight hours. Arthur Lee accused him of spying, but because Benjamin Franklin's faith never wavered the double agent with the credentials of a scholar probably did more than any other one man to prolong the American struggle for independence.

His Excellency, George Washington

Titles and terms of address long familiar in England and hence to English colonists were not easily discarded, even after leaders reached a decision to risk all in open war. From the day he was named head of the American fighting force, Washington frequently got—though he never sought—the title of "Excellency."

A typical reference appears in a June 12, 1776, letter of Colonel Loammi Baldwin to his wife Mary.

"We are in dayly expectation of the enimy," he wrote to her from headquarters at North River, New York. "Our works go on well. His Excellency returned from Congress about five days ago, but nothing very material of his business has transpired."

Baldwin didn't explain to his wife whom he meant by the term; it was not necessary. Throughout the colonies, great numbers of civilians and fighting men alike persisted in dubbing Washington as "His Excellency" or "Your Excellency."

Washington discouraged use of the title, but he was powerless to stop it. He frequently referred to himself in third person (especially when issuing general orders), much in the fashion of European monarchs. But the title that Washington typically called himself was "the General."

Years later, when he was named the first head of a nation gradually formed out of a cluster of independent states, he found himself still struggling with the matter of title. Many citizens considered "the President" a title lacking in dignity and persisted in using "His Excellency" to name the head of a democratic nation in which—theoretically—every citizen is on a par with every other citizen.

Colonel Laommi Baldwin, 26th Massachusetts

Colonel Laommi Baldwin of the 26th Massachusetts regiment saw action early and remained in uniform much longer than many other patriots. His most important contribution to the story of the Revolution, though, was a series of letters written to his wife.

Ordered to New York, the officer found streets of the city "not so fine as those in Boston." He noted, too, that manners of citizens "differ something from the natural inhabitants of Boston, having Jewish, Dutch and Irish customs."

More than anything else, Baldwin disliked the open immorality of the sprawling city. Writing to his wife on June 12, 1776, he reported that prostitution flourished openly and seemed to be very lucrative. Then he hastened to add that he himself had been careful to avoid contact with whores of the metropolis.

"Perhaps you will call me censorious and exclaim too much upon bare reports when I say that I was never within the door of nor 'changed a word with any of them except in the execution of my duty as officer of the day in going the grand round with my guard of escort," he wrote. "I have broke up the knots of men and women fighting, pulling caps, swearing, crying 'Murder' etc.—hurried them off to the Provost dungeon by half dozens, there let them lay mixed till next day. Then some are punished and sum get off clear—Hell's work."

Undistinguished as he was in battle, letter-writer Baldwin had an exceptionally green thumb. After taking off his uniform he devoted himself to horticulture and developed the Baldwin apple—long famous as the standard winter apple of eastern America and until modern times more widely grown than any other American apple.

First American Soldier to Be Executed

Little is known about the early life of Thomas Hickey. Relatively early in the conflict with England he enlisted in the Continental Army—where he soon saw what he considered to be an opportunity for a huge windfall.

Through intermediaries, Hickey plotted with Sir William Howe to carry out a daring exploit. As a guardsman, Hickey felt that he could get access to George Washington. So he contracted to seize the commander in chief and deliver him to the British under cover of night.

The plot never got off the ground, however. Hickey was placed under military arrest and became the subject of the first military trial in U. S. history. Convicted, he was ordered to forfeit his life for his deeds.

On June 27, 1776, in New York City, officers and men of the Spencer, Heath, Sterling, and Scott brigades were assembled under arms at their barracks They then marched to the execution place near Bowery Lane, which they reached about 10:00 A.M.

In the presence of about 20,000 spectators the first American soldier to be executed as a result of a court-martial was hanged on a gibbet that employed the relatively new "short drop" that was considered to be both efficient and merciful.

The People Versus the King

In drafting the Declaration of Independence, Thomas Jefferson was careful to emphasize the fact that rebels quarreled not with the mother country as such, but with the king of that country.

"The history of the present King of Great Britain is a history of repeated injuries and usurpations, all having in direct object the establishment of an absolute Tyranny over these States," said Jefferson. He then listed grievances that began, "He has refused his Assent to Laws, the most wholesome and necessary for the public good." One after another, the charges began with "He": King George III himself.

That assessment of the situation was brilliantly accurate. Contemporary English observers noted that "few wars in history have been initiated against such violent opposition." Not only merchants who feared the loss of American accounts, but veteran fighting men who knew the problems of mounting an attack three thousand miles overseas, advised the king to placate angry colonists and come to terms with them.

Adjutant General Harvey, senior staff officer in Whitehall, gave as his formal opinion the verdict that any attempt to conquer America by force was "as wild an idea as ever contraverted common sense." Even the noted *Annual Register* (1777) solemnly told its readers that "the penal laws . . . and the act called the Military Bill . . . brought results very different from those intended." Instead of putting an end to trouble, the stiff punishments simply stiffened the spirit of opposition.

But King George III (who had experienced his first violent attack of mental illness in 1765) was the formal head of the nation's military forces, and he was determined not to be dismayed "by any difficulties that may arise on either side of the Atlantic." Identification of George III as the chief foe of America in the debate preceding adoption of the Declaration of Independence was almost uncannily accurate.

Congress Deletes an Attack

Formal adoption of the Declaration of Independence meant that the document was signed by just one man—John Hancock, the presiding officer. Four days later it was read publicly in Independence Square, Philadelphia.

But the document Hancock signed on what came to be celebrated as the day of national independence was quite different in one aspect from Jefferson's draft. Debate that began on June 28 and continued for several days had led to deletion of an entire section.

Though he was himself an owner of slaves, Jefferson had included an eloquent attack upon the institution of Negro slavery—blaming the king of England for its existence in the colonies. At the specific direction of Congress, the following little-known segment of the original Declaration of Independence was not part of the document as offically adopted.

He [King George III] has waged cruel war against human nature itself, violating its most sacred rights of life and liberty in the persons of a distant people who never offended him, captivating and carrying them into slavery in another hemisphere, or to incur miserable death in their transportation thither. This piratical warfare the opprobrium of *infidel* powers, is the warfare of the *Christian* king of Great Britain. Determined to keep open a market where MEN should be bought and sold, he has prostituted his negative for suppressing every legislative attempt to suppress or restrain this execrable commerce; and that this assemblage of horrors might want no fact of distinguished die, he is now exciting these very people to rise in arms among us, and to purchase that liberty of which *he* deprived them, by murdering the people upon whom *he* also obtruded them; thus paying off former crimes committed against the *liberties* of one people, with crimes which he urges them to commit against the *lives* of another."

Adoption of the Jefferson clause, say historians, might have prevented the U.S. Civil War by eliminating slavery in the new nation.

Bullets for Rebels from King George III

Continental soldiers quartered in New York were under no delusions. British forces were already showing signs of moving toward the strategic center. The climate of tension added to the drama enacted on July 9, 1776. That day Continental troops stood at attention to hear for the first time the reading of the Declaration of Independence.

Once the cheering had subsided and troops had been dismissed, many soldiers began to think about King George III. The monarch, mentioned many times in the Declaration of Independence as chief villain of the struggle getting under way, had dominated New York for six years.

Not in person, of course, but by means of a splendid equestrian statue made in London by Joseph Wilton and erected on a marble pedestal in Bowling Green. There are no contemporary records to indicate who first thought of doing away with the king, but observers and participants said that before evening, "a vast throng" had gathered before the four-thousand-pound statue.

Toppled from place by men tugging on ropes, it was immediately attacked. One band of patriots sawed the head off the lead figure while musicians played "The Rogue's March"—traditionally used when a rogue was about to be tarred and feathered. Patriots probably planned to place the head on a pike and display it as a trophy.

Many of the larger pieces were put aboard a fast ship and sent to a Connecticut port, then transported overland to Litchfield where the most efficient Continental military depot was already busy turning out bullets. Lead from the statue of King George yielded precisely 42,088 bullets—most or all of which were eventually fired at His Majesty's troops.

Hotbed of Loyalty

New York, castigated by patriots as a hotbed of loyalty, probably had no greater percent of Tories than other colonies. But concentration of population there made the emergence of Loyalists more obvious and alarming than in thinly populated regions.

During the conflict, at least 15,000 New Yorkers (the majority of them coming from New York City) enlisted in the British Army and in the British Navy. Loyalists provided an additional 8,000 or so militia whose companies and regiments were under the command of British officers.

Since the thirteen former colonies provided, all together, only about 50,000 fighting men—regular or militia—who took up arms against their fellow countrymen, New York was responsible for nearly half of all loyalists who donned uniforms.

In this hotbed of struggle and intrigue, seesawing back and forth between American and British control, it was natural that some loyalists should seize what they saw as an opportunity for personal advancement. One such person was Mayor David Mathews of New York City. He not only worked actively for the British cause from August, 1776, until the Continentals became permanent masters of the city but he also masterminded an abortive attempt to kidnap George Washington. Mathews himself referred to the matter as "tampering with the general's guards"—who dutifully accepted bribes offered by Mathews' agents, then informed Washington of what was taking place.

Lord Stirling, American Hero

Several European noblemen came to the aid of patriots in North America and made such an impact that their names are household words. But one gallant fighter who bore a fancy title is all but forgotten.

William Alexander of New York came to Washington's attention early in the conflict. A seasoned military leader, he was noted chiefly for the fact that he was claimant to the Scottish title of Earl of Stirling. Though he was an early general in the Continental Army, he was most often referred to simply as Lord Stirling.

During the battle of Long Island in August, 1776, Lord Stirling was involved in action as dramatic and heroic as that celebrated in the famous poem about the charge of the Light Brigade.

Hopelessly outnumbered and lacking weapons with which to stand up against British firepower, Continental forces wavered and their foes prepared to cut them to pieces. In this emergency, Lord Stirling sent the bulk of his men on a hasty but orderly retreat. He remained with Major Mordecai Gist and 250 Marylanders to cover the retreat.

But instead of slowly giving ground, Stirling led his tiny band in wave after wave of attacks. They made at least five assaults against Hessian troops supported by grenadiers and bought enough time to enable great numbers of patriots to find their way to safe ground. After having "fought like a wolf" Lord Stirling was captured. Of the Marylanders whom he led in the rearguard action, only Mordecai Gist and nine others succeeded in fighting their way back to Continental lines.

From Thomas Jefferson's Head

One June 10, 1776, many members of the Continental Congress viewed with alarm a resolution proposing that the colonies declare their complete independence from the mother country. Postponing action, a committee was named to draft a document for consideration. Five men were appointed to serve on the committee: John Adams, Benjamin Franklin, Thomas Jefferson, Robert Livingston, and Roger Sherman.

Almost at once they agreed that the proposed document would have to be the work of one man. Thomas Jefferson, just thirty-three years old, was a relative newcomer to the Congress and was among its youngest members. But he had already made a reputation for clear thinking, and his colleagues on the special committee insisted that he do the work of drafting the document.

Years later (writing from Monticello on August 30, 1823) Jefferson told James Madison that the committee of five "unanimously pressed on myself alone to undertake the draught." Recalling the tension-filled period in which it was prepared, Jefferson insisted that he really didn't know whether he drew his ideas and phrases from earlier reading or from long meditation; "I only know that I turned to neither book nor pamphlet while writing it."

Congress voted for independence on July 2—by one of the few unanimous votes of that body. Then Jefferson's document —modified slightly at the suggestion of Franklin and Adams —was debated clause by clause. After substantial changes it was adopted on July 4. But it didn't take the status of a legal document until formal "signing" by delegates began on August 2. Signed or not, hastily printed copies had already been circulated far and wide, so that the Declaration of Independence was accepted as the chief document of American freedom before signatures of delegates made it legal.

The Burning of New York

Late in August, 1775, British forces under Howe and his fellow commanders showed themselves vastly superior to the Continentals. Measured by any standard, the battle of Long Island was a disaster for the patriots. There was no choice; the city of New York would have to be abandoned.

Washington, who had seen the inevitable coming, had earlier proposed that the city be burned. This, he pointed out, would effectively reduce its strategic value to the British. Congress gave little heed to the proposal; it had few supporters, even among Washington's closest friends and admirers.

Only weeks after Howe's troops had occupied the port city it suffered a disastrous fire. Both patriots and loyalists suffered heavy losses, for a large part of New York went up in flames.

Pondering the turn of events, the American commander in chief found it hard to restrain his elation. Writing to his cousin, Washington summed up the burning of New York City in a single sentence that—as much as his battlefield exploits—showed his total commitment to a fight to the finish.

"Providence," he said of the blaze that levelled much of the city, "or some good honest fellow, has done more for us than we were disposed to do for ourselves."

John Glover's 21st Massachusetts

In early life, John Glover was a shoemaker. Living in Marblehead, Massachusetts, he saved enough money to become a fish vender. Earnings from this business were sufficient to set him up as a merchant, and he became a man of wealth. Until after the Boston Tea Party—which effectively demonstrated the financial implications of the growing struggle—Glover showed little interest in military affairs.

He had, however, been trained as an officer in the local militia. So when war began he was promoted to the rank of colonel and authorized to raise volunteers who would form the 21st Massachusetts Regiment. Many of Glover's recruits were veterans of the sea; he had already made a name for himself as a master of business strategy.

So it was to Glover and his 21st regiment that George Washington turned when events during the Battle of Long Island made it clear that Continental troops would have to escape by sea if they expected to avoid death or capture. Glover and his men executed so skillful an evacuation during August 29-30, 1776, that Washington was left with a fighting force that might otherwise have been lost—and with it the Revolution.

Glover and his vital 21st Massachusets Regiment again supervised transportation in December of that year. This time moving toward attack rather than effecting a retreat, the unit commandeered and then helped to man the boats in which Washington and his men crossed the Delaware in order to take their foes by surprise at Trenton, New Jersey.

No other unit in the entire Continental land or naval forces matched the role of the 21st Massachusetts in its record of two dangerous but successful movements of large numbers of troops by water.

The *American Turtle*

David Bushnell of Saybrook, Connecticut, envisioned a craft capable of underwater attack upon enemy shipping and succeeded in completing a trial model late in 1775. A one-man craft that was six feet high and equipped with hand-cranked propellers, it looked enough like a turtle to warrant its name.

Bushnell, a graduate of Yale College, gave the "infernal vessel" a trial run in the Connecticut River—then offered it to the Continental Army. General Samuel H. Parsons became interested in it and personally called for volunteers to learn how to operate the *Turtle*.

Sergeant Ezra Lee of Lyme, Connecticut, was chosen to test the clumsy submarine under combat conditions. He found that when it was on the surface, he could get plenty of air from the two tubes provided for the purpose by inventor Bushnell. But when submerged, the *Turtle* had only enough oxygen to last half an hour.

On the night of September 7, 1776, the intrepid submarine commander strapped himself into the machine. Two whaleboats towed the vessel toward the British fleet anchored in New York harbor just north of Staten Island. Lee submerged his craft and set out to blow a British battleship out of the water.

He succeeded in reaching a vessel that he identified as H.M.S. *Eagle*, huge flagship of Lord Howe. Now Lee had only to operate his gear, attach an oak-sheathed time bomb loaded with 130 pounds of gunpowder, and make his getaway. He would have succeeded, he later explained, except for one fact. His wood-boring bit, which he expected to use to attach the bomb to the warship, simply wouldn't cut through thick copper sheathing of H.M.S. *Eagle*.

Thwarted in history's first submarine assault, Lee returned to patriot lines to receive congratulations from General Washington himself. The *American Turtle* was used as a surface craft a few times, then scrapped.

Ribbands, Cockades, and Knots

Though formally constituted by authority of the Continental Congress, the troops provided for George Washington were a motley lot. A few units that had been privately recruited were furnished with uniforms; most men simply went to war in whatever clothing they had. Eventually the drab appearance of these troops was to prove an advantage in battle, but at least during early weeks of organization and training the use of civilian dress created many problems.

One of them was the tendency of soldiers to treat everyone alike. There was no way by which a man could at a glance determine whether he was approaching an ordinary infantryman or an officer. Many patriots were not enthusiastic about taking commands from officers under any circumstances.

Washington pondered the situation and found it intolerable. One of his earliest general orders was designed to get rid of the pervasive spirit of total democracy under which no army could hope to function.

For himself, Washington arranged to secure "a light blue Ribband, to be worn across the breast, between Coat and Waistcoat." Major generals were provided with purple ribbands; brigadiers got pink ones; and aides de camp had green ones. There is no record that any other Continental officer was reimbursed for the cost of the ribband showing his rank, but Washington's now famous expense account shows that he charged the nation three shillings and fourpence for his personal insignia.

Cockades were sent to field officers—yellow ones for captains and green ones for subalterns. Sergeants had to settle for shoulder knots of red cloth, while corporals donned green ones.

Crude as it was by comparison with the splendid symbols used by his foes, Washington's system of ribbands, cockades, and knots helped transform a crowd of volunteers into a structured army in which the chain of command could function.

The Mystery of Patrick Ferguson

Born in Scotland in 1744, Patrick Ferguson enlisted in the British army very early and became a specialist in firearms. "Brown Bess," the standard British weapon of the era, was cumbersome and inaccurate. The fourteen-pound piece had an effective range of about eighty yards.

Ferguson developed a light-weight, breech-loading weapon that he hoped would win the world for Britain. It weighed only seven and a half pounds, fired six shots per minute, and had an effective range of three hundred yards—nearly four times that of the "Brown Bess" that took its name from Queen Elizabeth.

Ferguson gave a special demonstration before King George III and made such an impressive showing that he won a royal commission sending him to North America to recruit and train a sharpshooters' corps. Attached to Howe's force, Ferguson's little band of riflemen—far the most deadly in the entire British Army—marched into Pennsylvania in September, 1776.

On September 7 Ferguson and three of his sharpshooters were ranging far ahead of British lines. They heard horses coming and took cover. Soon they spotted two approaching rebels—one mounted on a bay horse and wearing "a remarkable cocked hat." Ferguson had never seen George Washington face to face, but woodcuts and prints of the rebel commander were plentiful.

The British officer signaled his men to prepare to fire—then suddenly reversed his decision. George Washington and his aide trotted casually out of range. Ferguson later wrote that he "could have lodged half of dozen of balls in or about him before he was out my reach." Why didn't he? The nearest he ever came to explaining why he let Washington live was that "it is not pleasant to fire at a man's back." Disregarding the mission for which he had come to America and restrained by factors he himself never made articulate, Patrick Ferguson changed the course of history by holding his fire.

A Tea Party at Inclenberg Farm

Tablets erected by the Mary Murray and the Knickerbocker Chapter, Daughters of the American Revolution, mark otherwise forgotten Inclenberg Farm. Now located approximately at Park Avenue and 37th Sreet, in New York City, the farm was once owned by prosperous planter-merchant Robert Murray.

Soon after General William Howe became commander in chief of British forces in 1776, he developed plans for the New York campaign. He expected to use sea power to the fullest, got the promise of 30,000 men and a great number of ships from his brother, Admiral Richard Howe.

George Washington, who had assumed command of armed forces of the colonies, had only 17,000 men on Long Island and Manhattan. Many of them had never seen battle. When it was obvious that the British were coming, Washington feared that his whole army might be captured. He suggested that New York be burned so it would not fall into British hands, but that idea was vetoed.

On September 13, 1776, the British launched a combined land and sea operation calculated to trap the main body of the Continental Army. Washington's subordinate, General Israel Putnam, ordered his men to retreat. Nature of the terrain and proximity of the enemy slowed their movements, and for a few hours it appeared that they couldn't get off the island.

Mrs. Mary Lindley Murray saw the British coming and hurriedly arranged a tea party for General Howe and his officers. Some historians think Howe had no orders to go beyond Inclenberg. Whether that's the case or not, he and his officers did sip Mrs. Murray's tea long enough for Colonial forces directly in his line of march to escape through Harlem Heights. Men who got away while the British drank tea later helped send their foes home, defeated.

New Settlers for Pennsylvania

Withdrawal of Continental forces from New York City in September, 1776, left patriots in a precarious position. Even among the most ardent foes of the king, many felt that the attempt to throw off England's yoke had been made too soon and could only end in a quick defeat.

It was in this climate that a Philadelphia baker volunteered for one of the most dangerous missions of the war. Born about 1720 in the German state of Hesse-Darmstadt, Christopher Ludwick had served in the Prussian army before deciding to try his luck in the new world. He was such an ardent patriot that in an early public meeting where subscriptions were being taken for purchase of firearms, he rose and said, "Although I am but a poor gingerbread baker, put me down for two hundred pounds!"

In October, 1776, he suggested to George Washington that he be permitted to go to New York in disguise. Once there, he was confident that he could persuade many of his fellow Germans to desert.

No one knows how many trips Ludwick made back and forth between the lines or the precise number of trained fighting men he drained from British forces occupying New York. This much is certain: he got his recruits by persuading them to go to Pennsylvania to become settlers. Several hundred actually made the dangerous journey, and renounced their citizenship in order to become Americans.

At the time of Ludwick's death in 1801, Dr. Benjamin Rush lauded his little-known exploits and described the new settlers he found for Pennsylvania as "now in comfortable freeholds or on valuable farms, with numerous descendants, and they bless the name of Christopher Ludwick."

Soldiers Turned Sailors Bought Time

Within weeks after the Declaration of Independence was issued, astute patriots found clues suggesting that the British would invade New York by way of Lake Champlain. Scouts and spies reported having seen activities that suggested men-of-war were designed for the inland waterways. Big vessels were being sailed up the St. Lawrence River to the rapids and dismantled there. There could be but one objective: moved overland in pieces, the ships would be rebuilt and used to move British forces toward New York.

Rebel leaders responded by launching a ship-building program of their own on Lake Champlain. By early fall, they had fifteen crudely constructed ships—and knew that the *Inflexible*, the *Carleton*, the *Maria,* and perhaps other fine ships originally built in England had been prepared as the nucleus of a British fresh-water navy. Benedict Arnold was given the job of stopping the invasion.

"They are a miserable set," he wrote of his sailors after taking his first look at them. "The marines are the refuse of every regiment, and the seamen, few of them were ever wet with salt water."

His verdict was right. Practically all of the American sailors had been sent to join the fleet by officers who wanted to be rid of troublemakers or idlers.

Seven hundred of these motley sailors faced an equal number of veteran British tars. In a running battle that began at Valcour Island on October 11, America's inland navy lost two-thirds of her ships and about 90 percent of the men who made up their crews. Valcour Island is now largely forgotten. But naval historian Alfred T. Mahan insists that these soldiers turned sailors bought for colonists a full year's time—a crucial year that led to the surrender of Burgoyne and the decision of France not to aid Britain in quelling the rebellion.

Kidnappers on the Prowl

Before and during the long years of armed warfare between conflicting groups each of whom claimed civilian as well as military members, both loyalists and patriots were engaged in kidnap plots. A few succeeded; most did not.

Richard Stockton, a signer of the Declaration of Independence, was successfully taken by a band of New Jersey Tories in November, 1776. Most such undertakings were not skillfully executed, but were aimed at top leaders on both sides.

Colonel Banastre Tarleton, a notorious loyalist who gained infamy in the South Carolina campaigns, made a personal trip to Virginia in order to mastermind an attempt to kidnap Thomas Jefferson. Joseph Galloway, an otherwise undistinguished and practically unknown Tory, set out to kidnap Governor William Livingston of New Jersey. When that effort failed, he laid plans—never set into execution—to kidnap the entire Continental Congress.

George Washington was the target of a famous plot in the summer of 1776. Governor Tryon of New York and Mayor David Mathews of New York City were co-conspirators in a well-planned attempt to kidnap Washington. It was foiled because a hastily written letter fell into patriot hands.

Long afterward the intended victim himself became the planner of another kidnapping that also failed. George Washington, infuriated at the actions of Benedict Arnold and aware that the traitor was beyond military reach in his New York City haven, almost—but not quite—succeeded in kidnapping the one-time general of the Continental Army.

The King's Shilling

During the eighteenth century, the British military force was made up of two quite distinct groups. Officers sought the army as an avenue for an easy and an often lucrative career. Enlisted men received low pay and had little hope of advancement. As a result, recruitment was a perennial problem.

Statutes provided that any male who accepted one shilling from a recruitment officer was obligated to enter the army —where he might spend many years. A small number of men volunteered. Others were seized under compulsory enlistment acts that gave "press gangs" the right to seize and put into uniform "any fortune teller, any idle, unknown or suspected fellow in a parish."

Even the activity of press gangs didn't produce enough recruits. As a result, it became widely customary for an aggressive recruitment sergeant to spend part of his own pay and allowances on liquor. After finding a prospect—for whom he would receive a stipend from his own commanding officer—the recruitment sergeant tried to get the fellow drunk enough to accept from him a single shilling. Once this was done, there was no way to avoid military service.

A contemporary crusader, author of a widely circulated pamphlet, charged (probably correctly) that "by lies they lured them, by liquor they tempted them, and when they were dead drunk they forced a shilling into their fist."

Many—but not all—enlisted men who served in North America entered the British Army by accepting the King's Shilling. For these men, it was far more important to avoid punishment by officers than to defeat rebels.

John Honeyman, Spy

At first look, a brawny Scotch-Irish weaver wouldn't appear to be a likely candidate for the role of spy—much less a double agent.

Yet just such a man played a vital role in events that gave patriots their first real morale boost after the heady days in which the Declaration of Independence was adopted.

For five months, Colonial forces failed to halt the advance of professional soldiers from Europe. George Washington himself became so discouraged that on December 18, 1776, he wrote to his brother that "I think the game is pretty near up." His ragged, hungry, and cold men were close to the point of mutiny.

Washington had just one real chance—if he could oust the Hessian troops who occupied the important town of Trenton, New Jersey, the tide of the war might turn. But in order to penetrate Trenton he needed help. A double agent who would feed false information to the enemy and simultaneously keep patriots informed about activities in Trenton was vital to the plan. Such a job was so dangerous that the commander in chief penned a special order dated simply "American Camp, Nov., A.D.1776."

The order was for the protection of "the wife and children of John Honeyman, the notorious Tory, now within the British lines, and probably acting the part of a spy."

Posing as a butcher, Honeyman gained the confidence of leaders of the forces of occupation. He managed to give Washington information vital to a surprise attack upon Trenton—then had to flee because patriots believed him to be a Tory. Only the fact that Washington had ordered his family to be protected saved Honeyman's wife and children from the wrath of fellow countrymen who didn't know he was actually working for their cause.

Cannoneer in Skirts

Born on the Pennsylvania frontier in 1751, a girl of five became an orphan when her father was killed by Indians and her mother was carried off into captivity. Just how little Margaret, or Molly, escaped with her life is unknown.

At age twenty-one she married Virginia farmer John Corbin and for a time played the role of housewife. She refused to stay at home, though, when her husband enlisted in Captain Thomas Proctor's First Company of Pennsylvania Artillery. With a few other women who were camp followers to their fighting husbands, she watched the near degeneration of Continental forces under a series of smashing blows by British troops.

John Corbin served as a matross, or cannoneer, who loaded and then fired a heavy gun. His wife watched the sequence of movements frequently enough to become thoroughly familiar with them.

Proctor's Artillery was among the units left to hold isolated Fort Washington in northern Manhattan when Continental forces began retreating from the area. British attacking forces who moved against the fort outnumbered Continentals by at least five to one. They had the additional advantage of artillery heavier than anything yet available to patriots—plus big guns on warships in the Hudson River.

Colonel Magaw, commander of the fort, defiantly refused Howe's November 15 demand for surrender, so British big guns moved forward in force. Early in the action a cannoneer was killed, so Molly Corbin—skirts and all—took his place and managed to get off blast after blast at the British. Her husband was killed, and she was badly wounded by grape shot before becoming a prisoner of war. When peace came she dubbed herself "Captain Molly" in spite of the fact that she never wore a uniform; she received from Congress half the pay of a private for life and a direct grant from the State of Pennsylvania in the amount of thirty dollars.

A Country Rich in Plunder

Though comparatively unknown in the light of contests at Concord and Lexington, Bunker Hill and Yorktown, the Battle of Fort Washington was one of the most costly of the entire war. Patriots under the command of General Nathaneal Greene held a practically useless fort on Manhattan Island. Hessian troops broke the back of American defenses and turned the battle into carnage.

Loyalists who heard about activities of the day often cheered at word that the German mercenaries had stripped captured Continental soldiers of their clothing. It was generally known that these professional soldiers from Europe had been told before leaving home that they would go to a land rich in plunder—and that captured goods would exceed the value of their pay and allowances.

What few loyalists knew in the aftermath of British victory at Fort Washington was that the typical Hessian soldier spoke little or no English. This had an effect not anticipated by leaders on either side of the conflict.

Loyalists who took oaths of allegiance to England and the king were given certificates which were supposed to render them immune from plundering by British forces. But since Hessians couldn't read the documents, their protective value vanished. Especially in New Jersey, farms and shops and homes of many loyalists were literally stripped by soldiers of the king's army. Cattle and sheep were killed on the spot or driven off. Furniture and clothing were seized. Even churches were sacked.

Having been ordered to serve in a conflict about which they knew little and probably cared less, Hessians made the most of the promise of "a country rich in plunder"—and seldom tried to distinguish between rebels and loyalists.

More Deadly than British Bullets

Relatively early in the struggle, patriots learned that it was better to risk death in battle than to surrender. Totally unprepared to house or to feed large numbers of prisoners, the British adopted whatever makeshift measures they could.

One expedient was the use of rotting ships as prisons. American evacuation of New York City in 1776 gave the British a splendid base of operations—plus plenty of water in which to moor vessels crowded with men who had laid down their arms in battle.

According to historian Henry Steele Commager, "the British prison ships probably killed more American soldiers than British rifles: the total estimate runs to 7,000 or 8,000."

Most prison ships were concentrated near New York; many were anchored off the beach of what is now Brooklyn. Escape was all but impossible because the water barrier was more effective than iron bars or stone walls.

A few hardy men spent two, three, or even four years on prison ships—and lived to tell of them. Their journals and diaries are full of brief entries that have a poignancy much like concentration camp documents of World War II:

"Thursday, 21st (November, 1776). We passed the day in sorrow having nothing to eat or drink but pump water."

"Saturday, 7th. We drew 4 lb. of bisd [biscuit] at noon."

"Sunday, 15th. Drawed bisd. Paleness attends all faces. The melancholyst day I ever saw."

"Sunday, 22nd. Last night nothing but grones all night of sick and dying. Deaths multiply. Drawed bisd. All faces sad."

A Noble Volunteer at Nineteen

Marie Joseph Paul Yves Roch Gilbert du Motier is not familiar to Americans—but the Marquis de Lafayette is. The two names indicate a single man.

Born at Chavaniac on September 6, 1757, Lafayette lost his parents when he was very young. So by the time he married Adrienne de Noailles when he was sixteen, the Marquis was a wealthy man. He purchased a captain's commission in the Noailles dragoons, but found French military life of the period boring.

Partly because he was personally restless, largely because he was inspired by the sentiments of revolutionary writers in America, he approached the American agent in Paris. In December, 1776, at age nineteen, the Marquis de Lafayette secured from Silas Deane a commission as major general in the Continental army.

Both King Louis XVI and Lafayette's father-in-law tried to persuade him to give up foolish ideas about becoming a hero in North America, but nothing would stop the young adventurer. He reached Philadelphia on July 27, 1777, and presented his credentials. Congress (rather reluctantly) conceded that the commission of its own agent would have to be honored, so they confirmed the arrangement by which the Frenchman would become a major general. But the Congressional documents stipulated that he must serve as a "volunteer"—at his own expense and without a command.

Lafayette endeared himself to Washington, distinguished himself at the Battle of Brandywine (September 11, 1777), and eventually got his own command. Before the struggle ended, he had become the symbol of Franco-American friendship, a potent force not only on the battlefield but also at conference tables. His own grateful nation promoted him to the rank of *marechal de camp* (or major-general), the rank conferred upon a youthful volunteer years earlier by Silas Deane.

Captured by His Own Men

English-born Charles Lee, a soldier of fortune who was willing to sell his services to the highest bidder, had the doubtful distinction of being the only Revolutionary general to be captured by men he had once commanded.

As a colonel in the British Army he had a tour of duty in Portugal, where he commanded the 16th Dragoons. Back in England in 1763, with no major war brewing, he felt that he would do better for himself in civilian life than in the military. So he resigned his commission and took half pay.

After adventures in Poland and in Turkey, he went to America (which he had visited earlier) and took up land in Berkeley County, Virginia. There is some evidence that he still had grandiose plans about establishing a new British colony in the Illinois country.

But the outbreak of open hostilities offered the veteran adventurer-soldier what seemed a golden opportunity. He managed to win appointment on June 17, 1776, to the rank of major general of the Continental Army. Because of his English background, he insisted that Congress compensate him for any losses he might sustain from confiscation of his English holdings,

Erratic and vain, Lee was not a good commander. Late in 1776 he stepped up a campaign attacking General Washington (whom he hoped to replace as commander in chief). On December 12 he wrote a famous letter to General Gates, remarking confidentially that "between us, a certain great man is most damnably deficient."

On the very next day, Colonel Harcourt's 16th Dragoons rushed the Continental post and the men whom Lee had commanded in Portugal took him prisoner. He was kept in close confinement for a year, during which time he drafted plans aimed at showing the British how to defeat the Americans—papers that did not come to light until 1858 in order to give conclusive evidence that General Lee was prepared to serve anyone who would pay him well.

Washington Crosses the Delaware

For generations, Emanuel Leutze's "Washington Crossing the Delaware" has remained among the two or three most popular paintings about the Revolution. It has hung on tens of thousands of schoolroom walls, appears in history books and biographies of our first President, and is perennially popular as an engraving.

Practically everything about the famous picture is wrong, though.

It was done in Dusseldorf, Germany, and first exhibited in the United States in 1851. Critics writing for New York's *Evening Mirror* called the huge (21' 4" by 12' 5") canvas "the grandest, most majestic, and most effective painting ever exhibited in America."

Leutze worked with only fragmentary information about the famous Battle of Trenton to which the crossing was a prelude. He had only Houdon's bust of Washington as a model for the commander in chief. And though he spent his early years in the United States, the artist was more concerned with creating a majestic scene than in depicting what actually happened.

Washington's own field orders indicate that the crossing did not take place in daylight as depicted; instead, boats embarked at "one hour before dawn."

The flag depicted in the famous painting hadn't been adopted in 1776. Journals of men who were present indicate that ice in the Delaware River was not nearly so formidable as it is represented. And to complete the list of indictments against the picture, it depicts the commander in chief standing boldly erect (rather than clutching a seat) while the boat lurches through treacherous waters. Washington did cross the Delaware and as a result did win his first big victory—but the passage wasn't remotely like it is depicted in one of our best-known historical paintings.

Hamilton's Lucky Shot

British troops who occupied the village of Princeton, New Jersey, during early weeks of 1777 were seasoned veterans. Most men came from three units: the 17th Leicestershires, the 40th South Lancashires, and the 55th Border Regiment. All three of these units had seen considerable action in North America—and many men were veterans whose lives had been spent in military service at home and in Europe.

Rank amateurs, in the military sense, set out to master them and take the town. Continental soldiers, most of whom used guns that were cumbersome and could be loaded only slowly, were no match for redcoats trained to use the bayonet in close combat. For a time it seemed that patriots would be driven off in confusion.

Arrival of George Washington changed the climate of the struggle. Continental soldiers gradually pressed against the British—many of whom took refuge in Nassau Hall, main building of the fledgling College of New Jersey. Behind walls of the relatively massive building, redcoats could hold out until reenforcements came.

Youthful Captain Alexander Hamilton, who was personally in charge of one of the few field pieces being used by patriots, had his cannon wheeled near Nassau Hall. He fired just one shot. Hamilton's ball, by chance, struck a portrait of King George II in the prayer hall and neatly decapitated the monarch.

Taking that as an omen, awed British regulars filed out of the big hall and handed over their arms to raw Continentals—some of whom were that day seeing their first battlefield action.

Hair-Buyer Hamilton

Lieutenant Colonel Henry Hamilton, commanding officer of the British post in the frontier town known as Detroit, knew he couldn't possibly beat rebel forces without help from American Indians. So he did what many officials in many wars have done. Using rum, trade trinkets, and blankets as bait he bought the loyalty of tribesmen, who were then supplied with muskets and ammunition.

Hamilton was neither worse nor better than French, British, and American officers of earlier periods who had employed precisely the same tactics. But with tempers already inflamed, his actions provided a splendid basis for propaganda against the enemy. Much evidence indicates that it was George Rogers Clark who in April, 1777, first dubbed the British soldier "Hair-Buyer Hamilton."

Though Hamilton clearly did promote Indian raids upon frontier settlements in Ohio, there is no evidence whatever that he actually offered prize money for scalps of patriots, their women and children. Clark's psychological attack was successful, however. For the remainder of his life (and even now in many reference works) the British soldier who simply did his duty as he understood it was known by the spine-chilling nickname bestowed upon him by a foe.

It was Hair-Buyer Hamilton who reacted to Clark's capture of Kaskaskia in French Illinois by marching to Vincennes, Indiana, to take command of the fort. So the 1779 surrender of the vital outpost was made to Clark by the man upon whom he had foisted a lasting nickname.

A New Military Elite

Daniel Morgan, born somewhere close to the Delaware River in 1736, was among the most zealous recruiters among the patriots. He hated the British with burning passion—because as a youthful soldier he had struck a British subaltern during the French and Indian Wars, and had been punished with five hundred lashes on his bare back.

Morgan won a commission as captain of a company of Virginia riflemen on June 22, 1775—then had to go out and find men to make up the company. He filled the ranks in just ten days, and three weeks later he reached Boston with his company intact after an overland march from Winchester, Virginia. Morgan and his men participated in Arnold's bold attempt to take Quebec, and as a reward for his courage and leadership in that campaign was promoted to colonel.

There are no documents to show whether it was George Washington who first proposed the idea of creating a new military elite or whether it was the man who still remembered those five hundred lashes. But Morgan and his commander in chief were in close consultation during the early spring of 1777. In April, Morgan organized a new corps—exactly five hundred sharpshooters (one for each lash he had received).

This elite corps was made up of men who already knew how to use rifles with deadly accuracy. Many Continental soldiers who carried muskets fired often but seldom hit a target. Morgan's Sharpshooters fired only when there was a reasonable chance of bringing down a redcoat. They rendered such signal service at the battles of Freeman's Farm and Bemis Heights that the idea was expanded, and special units of riflemen were incorporated into Continental forces wherever possible. To a degree far exceeding their numerical importance, these sharpshooters helped tip the scales in favor of American victory.

Sybil Ludington, Courier

More than two years after Paul Revere's ride that became world famous, patriots were still in need of couriers. Whenever word came that a British force was advancing, it was necessary to warn the countryside.

Such a message reached a Putnam County, New York, farm on the evening of April 27, 1777. A huge force of British regulars—estimated at two thousand in number—was on the march.

Sybil Ludington, sixteen-year-old daughter of a captain of the militia, volunteered to "arouse the countryside." Unlike Revere, she didn't have a fine riding horse—only a clumsy farm animal. But she climbed on his back and rode all night and through the early morning—covering a distance of about forty miles. Paul Revere rode an estimated fourteen miles before he was stopped outside Lexington by a British patrol and detained for questioning.

Word spread by the girl courier brought out enough minutemen and farmers to turn back the redcoats who retreated to their boats in confusion. But since no great master of literature has ever written a poem about Sybil Ludington (whose name, incidentally, doesn't lend itself to verse so readily as that of Paul Revere), she is virtually unknown.

Visitors to Putnam County—near the Connecticut state line —can now view a life-sized bronze statue erected a few years ago to the memory of the adolescent heroine. It shows her brandishing the heavy stick with which she pounded on cabin doors as she perched on her big horse, riding sidesaddle.

A Certificate of Loyalty

Whether native-born or born and reared in England, Americans never came close to full agreement about rejection of the king's authority. Numerous persons wavered back and forth between patriot and Tory camps of opinion. At least some of the time after active war was being waged, less than 50 percent of all colonists were in full support of the war for independence.

Great numbers of Tories, or loyalists who remained faithful to orders from the British crown, asked for and received certificates. Language of such certificates varied, but the intent of all was the same: to show that the bearer had remained true to England, and so would be immune from punishment or financial loss when His Majesty's troops had put down the rebellion.

David Mathews, Tory mayor of New York City, personally signed certificates of loyalty. Preprinted, the documents had blanks for insertion of names and dates. One such certificate, issued to otherwise unknown Tory David Brinkerhoff, informed all interested parties that:

I DO hereby Certify, That *David Brinkerhoff* has, in my presence voluntarily taken an OATH, to bear Faith and true Allegiance to HIS MAJESTY KING George the Third,—and to defend to the utmost of his Power, His sacred Person, Crown and Government, against all Persons whatsoever. Given under my Hand at New-York, this *15* Day of *May* in the Seventeenth Year of HIS MAJESTY'S reign, Anno. Dom. 1777. *D. Mathews* Mayor of the City of New-York.

Benjamin Rush, M.D.

Pennsylvania physician Benjamin Rush is remembered chiefly for his violent clashes with George Washington. But his real niche in history was gained as a result of extraordinary views about illness and medicine, formulated during his period of service in the Continental Army.

In 1777 Rush accepted the post of surgeon general of the armies of the Middle Department and almost immediately had a series of personality conflicts with other medical men. Rush protested to Washington who referred the matter to Congress. Congress refused to act on the recommendations of Rush, so the physician became an outspoken critic of the commander in chief and played an indirect role in the abortive conspiracy known as the Conway Cabal.

Dealing with great numbers of men and forced to make hasty decisions, Benjamin Rush began to formulate a new theory of illness. Although it didn't take final shape for some years, it was already being formulated before he resigned from the Continental Army in a huff.

Every malady to which man is subject, the physician concluded, stems from a single cause: a state of excessive "excitability," or spasm, in the blood vessels. Consequently he felt that any illness whatever should be treated by two methods: bleeding and purging. Under his direction, many a Continental soldier lost ten or more ounces of blood in a single treatment; sometimes three-fourths of the blood in the body was deliberately drained out.

To supplement his bleeding, the surgeon general used calomel (monochloride of mercury) in quantities that were huge even by standards of the era. Any patient who lost two or more pints of blood and then swallowed ten grains of calomel had to be made of iron to survive. Medical historian Byron Stinson calls the theories and practices of the Revolutionary physician "the absolute low point in the history of therapeutics."

Who Designed Old Glory?

Attempts to design a suitable flag for the rebellious colonies that were not yet a united nation proved to be far more difficult than might have been expected. The early Grand Union flag, which hinted at continuing ties with England, invited misunderstanding.

On June 14, 1777, Congress specified that the flag of the United States should be made up of "thirteen stripes alternate red and white" and "thirteen stars of white on a blue field." Even these specifications were so far from exact that a great variety of designs could have been shaped to meet them.

A young widow named Betsy Ross, "uncommonly seemly to the eye," is widely credited with having designed and produced the first flag of the type that unofficially came to be called Old Glory. Unfortunately, the charming tale is wholly without documentary support. It's in character, though, that Betsy Ross should be conceived as "uncommonly seemly"—for in legends and folk tales, the heroine is nearly always beautiful.

Slightly more evidence supports the claim made by a signer of the Declaration of Independence. Francis Hopkinson of Philadelphia put his claim in writing in 1780 and suggested that an appropriate reward for having designed his country's flag would be "a quarter-cask of the public wine." Later he revised his estimate upward and asked for a substantial payment.

After a congressional investigation, the claim was disallowed. But the influential *Dictionary of American Biography* still credits Hopkinson with having designed the flag in 1777.

Despite the loyalty of Betsy Ross and Francis Hopkinson adherents, the truth is that the flag so vaguely defined by Congress reached its final form at the hand of a person or persons who didn't bother to leave records.

Burgoyne's First Big Blunder

Documentary evidence is lacking, but many circumstances suggest that the first big blunder made by "Gentleman Johnny" Burgoyne was a concession to a shrewd war profiteer.

Philip Skene, one-time major in His Majesty's Forces, had laid claim to the vast wilderness area along the border of New York. His little village of Skenesborough was so isolated that it had little hope of attracting new settlers or artisans.

After the Battle of Ticonderoga in June, 1777, Burgoyne was eager to join forces with other British units then stationed in the vicinity of Albany, New York. He moved southward in haste and found himself at Skenesborough. Philip Skene, a genial and generous host, gave Burgoyne the best that he had. The two men, along with Burgoyne's advisors, talked long into the night of victories that lay ahead and laurels to be won.

From Skenesborough, Burgoyne logically should have taken a water route: Lake Champlain to Lake George, then to the Hudson River and Albany. But the overland route was a great deal shorter—just twenty-three miles to Fort Edward and civilization. At least, that's what Skene told him. He failed to add that the twenty-three mile route would take the British forces through virgin wilderness with trees so dense that even skilled Canadian woodsmen would be unable to keep a path cleared for troops.

History's verdict asserts that Skene persuaded Burgoyne to take the short overland route so that he could get a road built through his big and practically unexplored tract of forest land. Skene actually did get his road—and Burgoyne got a frustrating delay during which his troops moved forward at the rate of just one mile a day. That delay was enough to enable patriots to strengthen their own position as they waited for the British to come.

Jenny McCrea's Tresses

Leading an invasion of the colonies from Canada, General John Burgoyne had little difficulty taking Ft. Ticonderoga. He then proceeded south in order to seize Ft. Edward—already abandoned by patriots.

While Gentleman Johnny, as the British officer called himself, was camped on the trail toward Ft. Edward, a band of his American Indian allies brought to headquarters a trophy they particularly prized—a scalp with luxuriant tresses.

Burgoyne wanted to punish the braves in the war party responsible for the scalping, but feared that if he did so he would lose all of his Indian allies.

Patriots made Jenny McCrea's tresses a propaganda slogan aimed at proving that all British were heartless barbarians. Their cause was fostered by the fact that Jenny (or Jane) was not in defiance of the king as were some frontier women. Instead, she was the fiancée of Lt. David Jones, an officer in Colonel John Peters' band of loyal Tories.

There is some evidence that the girl was actually killed by a stray bullet, then scalped. But patriots painted a grim picture of fiends who employed red men to slay defenseless women—even among their own ranks. No frontier incident of the period did more to speed the pace of recruitment for the Continental Army than did the seizure of Jenny McCrea's long and beautiful hair.

Future Traitor Uses Dutch Turncoat

The flag now familiar as the Stars and Stripes was first raised against an enemy at Fort Stanwix (later renamed Fort Schuyler) on the Mohawk River, close to present-day Rome, New York. After a preliminary clash in early August, 1777, the fort's 750 defenders found themselves facing about 800 British regulars plus at least 1,000 American Indians.

Benedict Arnold, commander of the small force trying to save Fort Stanwix, sent scouting parties to capture as many loyalists as possible. One man who fell into the patriots' net was Dutch landed-proprietor Hon Yost Schuyler. Considered a lunatic by other whites of the region, Schuyler had adopted native dress and was regarded by many Indians as a great medicine man.

Arnold, according to the journal of Continental physician James Thacher, agreed that the settler "should be liberated and his estate secured to him on the condition that he would return to the enemy and make such exaggerated report of General Arnold's force as to alarm and put them to flight." These conditions were too good to refuse; the Dutch landowner became a turncoat and hurried to the pro-British force of American Indians. Aided by Oneida followers, Schuyler persuaded chieftains that the Great Spirit wanted the Indians to abandon the British. They accepted his message as authentic and withdrew in such haste that redcoats had no hope of taking the fort.

In this fashion, a Dutch turncoat given the strong-arm treatment by a future traitor played a crucial role in causing British to abandon their plans for Fort Stanwix and leave it with the Stars and Stripes still flying.

The Two-Month Army

Now a town in Vermont, the community of Bennington was originally chartered by New Hampshire and later claimed by New York. The town over which three states quarreled was an important supply base for Continental forces during 1776-77.

Expecting General Burgoyne to move his huge army toward the depot that held valuable stores, New Hampshire leaders knew that they could count on little or no help from the fledgling Continental Army. In this emergency, the state raised its own military force.

Speaker of the General Court John Langdon was the driving force behind the army that existed for just two months. In order to create it, he pledged his entire fortune—including his ancestral plate silver and the goods in his mercantile establishments. Brigadier General John Stark, personally unhappy with the way the Continental Army was being conducted, had taken off his uniform, but at Langdon's insistence he donned it again to lead New Hampshire's armed forces.

Stark led about 1,600 of New Hampshire's best—giving him a decided numerical advantage over the force of about 800 Tories, Canadians, Indians, and redcoats commanded by German Colonel Friedrich Baum. Still, the patriots were raw troops lacking in seasoning while the British force was made up of professionals.

In two separate engagements during August 15-16, 1777, Americans got the better of well-trained foes and took about 700 prisoners. Almost at once the threat of eastward movement by Burgoyne's main force vanished. After a life span of just two months the Army of New Hampshire was disbanded.

Washington on His Knees

One of the most familiar and best-loved incidents during the fearful stay of Continentals at Valley Forge, Pennsylvania, was reported by a Quaker. Known only as Potts but described as "a good and respectable Quaker," the civilian happened to pass through "a dark natural bower of ancient oaks" during the dreadful winter of 1777.

Reaching his cottage, Potts called to his wife: "Sarah, my dear! Sarah! All's well! All's well! George Washington will yet prevail! On his knees before the Heavenly Father, his face showed that his pleas were heard!"

Washington, according to the account, had retired to the bower for a period of solitary prayer to Almighty God that justice and freedom might prevail. He went without guards or aides, and the vivid incident might have gone unreported that it not been for the vigilant Mr. Potts.

Numerous post-Revolutionary artists painted their interpretations of the poignant scene, with the commander in chief upon his knees and looking up to heaven or bowed in humility.

There's only one serious flaw in the report of the incident.

It was first circulated by one-time parson Mason Weems, who turned his flair for writing into the profitable channel of preparing an ancedotal biography of George Washington. Weems is responsible for the famous story of the cherry tree about which little George could not tell a lie; that story has been traced to an English volume on *The Minstrel* (1799) from which the American adapted it for his own uses. If he lifted the account of a commander in chief going into the woods to pray, the source has never been uncovered—but neither has any evidence been found to support the tale about Washington (who actually had little use for religion or the church).

York, Pennsylvania, Our Forgotten Capital

Springett Penn, a grandson of William Penn, received in 1722 a grant of 64,000 acres in southeast Pennsylvania and promptly dubbed the region Springettsbury Manor. Until 1741 it had no settlement of importance, though. That year a village was laid out on Codorus Creek, a tributary of the Susquehanna river. Named for the English city of York, it boasted a population of nearly 1,000 by 1755.

British approach to Philadelphia in 1777 caused the Continental Congress to flee from the capital. Lawmakers paused in Lancaster for a single day's session, then reconvened in York. From September 30, 1777, to June 27, 1778, it was the capital of the nation that was coming into being.

Though seldom remembered as having been a national capital, York was the center of stirring and fateful activities.

It was here in the old county courthouse (torn down in 1849) that the Continental Congress adopted the Articles of Confederation. News of the surrender of Burgoyne reached lawmakers at York, and it was here that they also got word from Franklin that France would come to the aid of America.

Both Lafayette and von Steuben presented their credentials at York and both received their commissions as major generals in the tiny capital. Desperately needed silver from France in the sum of $1,500,000 reached York in September, 1778, but the hard money was not adequate to meet national needs. Benjamin Franklin transported a printing press from Philadelphia, and in York that press turned out an estimated $10,000,000 in Continental currency that soon became worthless.

General Howe's Dog

Smarting from their defeat at the hands of British in the Battle of Germantown on October 4, 1776, Washington and his troops withdrew in order to plan future strategy. With his senior officers, the commander in chief held a series of formal councils. Meanwhile, British forces under Sir William Howe were entrenched in nearby Philadelphia.

Late on the afternoon of October 6, the council of war had an unexpected interruption. A hunting dog trotted up to the group of officers and showed its fine training by standing quietly while its collar was examined.

The name on the collar identified the animal's owner as Sir William Howe.

Washington—himself a lover of animals—had the dog fed and groomed. Then, under a flag of truce, it was sent to Philadelphia for reunion with its master—presumably separated from him during the battle a few days days earlier.

Along with the dog, the commander in chief sent his foe a brief note: "General Washington's compliments to General Howe—does himself the pleasure to return him a dog which accidentally fell into his hands and, by the inscription on the collar, appears to belong to General Howe."

The Silver Bullet

General Sir Henry Clinton had reservations about ambitious plans of General Burgoyne, who had left London expecting to be back within eighteen months at most. Burgoyne was rash in Clinton's judgment. Still, he must be permitted to strike a few quick blows and thereby bring the American uprising to a speedy end.

Burgoyne proposed that his forces be joined with those of Clinton in order to crush resistance in strategically important New York.

Clinton boosted his comrade's chances for success by capture of Fort Montgomery on October 8, 1777. But he was too astute to think that the campaign was over. He wrote a brief summary —and warning—to Burgoyne: "Fort Montgomery, 8 October. *Nous voici* ["We are here"]—and nothing between us but [General] Gates. I sincerely hope this *little* success of ours may facilitate your operations. In answer to your letter of the 28th of September, I cannot presume to order, or even advise, for reasons obvious. I heartily wish you success."

General Burgoyne was to have received that message from Daniel Taylor who set out to deliver it to him in a hollow silver bullet. But Taylor was captured by Colonial forces. An officer saw him swallow something, so ordered that he be given a severe dose of emetic tartar. Dr. James Thacher, serving with the Continental Army, noted the incident in his journal. "This produced the happiest effect as respects the prescriber; but it proved fatal to the patient. He discharged a silver bullet, which being unscrewed, was found to enclose a letter from Sir Henry Clinton to Burgoyne."

By the time Burgoyne heard of the abortive attempt to send him good news, he himself had already surrendered with all of his men.

The
Wind Shifts

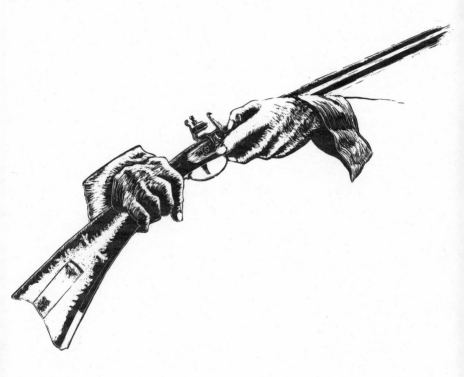

Defeated Hessians Kept New World Animals

General John Burgoyne, commander of a 1776 expedition sent from Canada against the American colonies, was rewarded by being placed at the head of more than 5,000 troops. About half of them were Hessians led by Baron Friederich von Riedesel; the rest were British regulars, "the King's finest," led by Major General William Phillips.

Continental forces, Burgoyne knew, were led by General Horatio Gates—whom the veteran British commander scornfully dubbed "the old midwife."

Assured by their leaders, who got the word from their commanding officer, Hessian mercenaries expected to be on ship for Europe before Christmas. Scores of them—officers as well as enlisted men—took native North American animals as prizes of war. Back home, these strange creatures would create a great sensation!

"The old midwife," General Gates, outwitted and out fought Burgoyne. Near the village of Saratoga (now Schuylerville) on the west bank of the Hudson River, Burgoyne's men laid down their arms on October 17, 1777.

Their American captors permitted the 2,412 Hessian prisoners to retain their personal belonging. As a result, some of them filed past ranks of Continental soldiers still leading their New World animals: bear cubs, usually but not always shackled; leashed foxes; young deer wearing halters; and racoons and other small animals in clumsy cages.

Whether any of the captured animals ever reached Germany is doubtful. For contrary to British predictions of a quick rebound, the surrender that involved animals of the forest as well as professional soldiers proved to mark what many analysts now regard as a turning point of the war—the beginning of the end for Britain and her mercenaries.

The Bogus Baron

Baron Friedrich Wilhelm Ludolf Gerhard Augustin von Steuben is universally known as "Drillmaster of the Continental Army." More than any other man, the Prussian who reached Washington's command post on December 1, 1777, was responsible for turning poorly organized and badly trained men into disciplined fighting troops.

What neither Washington nor any other American fighting man of the era knew was that the credentials of the baron were bogus. Precisely when and where his impressive dossier was made out for the purpose of making a great impression upon Congress, no one knows. This much is certain: von Steuben sailed to America from Paris with the wholehearted endorsement of Benjamin Franklin.

Many scholars believe that Franklin himself prepared the fake papers that were presented by the Prussian—or supervised their preparation. Whether that is the case or not, there is every reason to believe that the Sage of Philadelphia knew that von Steuben had been out of work for fourteen years and that he was actually a half-pay captain rather than a lieutenant general in the service of Frederick the Great of Prussia.

Some of the experts who are reasonably sure that Franklin himself had a hand in doctoring the credentials of the Prussian are most vocal in insisting that this may have been the greatest single service that he performed for his nation during the entire war. For though his rank and his credentials were bogus, von Steuben was a tough-minded drillmaster who managed to win the respect of men whose language he didn't speak and who in a matter of months boosted both the morale and the battle power of Washington's troops.

Fit Dress for Battle

Over a period of several centuries the etiquette of land warfare in Europe had come to prescribe leisurely preparations for battle often in full sight of the enemy followed by hand-to-hand conflict of large masses of men. Uniforms became increasingly elaborate, and clumsy, since opposing forces usually marched straight toward one another in formation and there was no need for garb that didn't stand out clearly.

British forces of the eighteenth century had adopted uniforms modelled after those already used in Germany. Infantrymen wore scarlet coats which had lavish decorations: facings, pipings, lace, and brass buttons. Long tails of these coats made a most imposing appearance during a dress parade.

High collars of coats were stiff, while hats were big and clumsy. In many units, boots weighed twelve pounds per pair even when not equipped with heavy spurs. The familiar "Brown Bess" musket that was the most widely used weapon of the British army weighed a full fourteen pounds. In addition to it, soldiers on the march carried packs that weighed 100 to 125 pounds.

"Fit dress for battle," a necessity in the eyes of men who had fought conventional battles in Europe, proved a major liability in the guerrilla warfare that waged in North America. Despite many paintings to the contrary, few American units were fully uniformed. Great numbers of Continentals took into battle the only clothing they had: drab homespun, buckskin, and the like. This gave them superb protective coloration, while the fancy uniforms of their opponents made them perfect targets against almost any background. Had the British not stubbornly persisted in dressing and fighting like gentlemen, their chances of ultimate victory would have been greatly enhanced.

The Great Chain

From the outset of armed clashes between Colonial and British forces, it was obvious that the Hudson River would play a vital role. If vessels of His Majesty's fleet could ascend it in sufficient numbers, they could separate New England from the rest of the colonies. This must not happen.

At least two blockades were established by patriots. One was made up of a barrier of ships deliberately scuttled in a fashion that would prevent British vessels from passing. But the water was too deep; sunken ships reached the bottom and listed over, so the enemy had no difficulty getting past the barrier.

An assault by means of fire ships was only a trifle more successful. Loaded with inflammable materials, half a dozen old sloops were set adrift in the river during August, 1776. They made contact with the British at Yonkers, tried to hold fast to enemy vessels with grappling hooks, and were set afire by members of their crew. Several British ships burned and sank—but sailors on the Continental vessels couldn't escape, either.

George Washington in December, 1777, ordered General Putnam to "exert every nerve in constructing and forwarding the proper works" with which to block British use of the Hudson. Putnam remembered that an 1800-foot chain had once stretched from bank to bank at St. Anthony's Nose, five miles south of West Point, but had broken under its own weight. Responding to the orders of his commander in chief, Putnam persuaded the Sterling Iron Works of New York to execute what he called "the great chain." Each of its two-foot links weighed 100 pounds. When installed, 2,000 men were sent to guard it. Though it apparently did its work well, even during part of the time that Benedict Arnold was in command at West Point, the great chain was eventually sold as scrap iron, and unless links still at West Point are original ones, none was preserved.

Military Dictatorship

During the entire period in which the Continental Congress limped along without real authority to govern the nation not yet actually formed, much that was done by George Washington smacked of military dictatorship. Theoretically subject to the authority of Congress, Washington actually acted in his capacity as commander in chief to get things done by any measures necessary.

Had he done otherwise, the Revolution would have come to a relatively quick and decisive end, with British rule more firmly established than ever.

But especially during crucial periods, the head of the Continental Army took actions far more drastic than any ever even attempted by the King's agents during years that preceded armed struggle.

December, 1777, represented just such a crucial period.

From his headquarters at Valley Forge on the twentieth day of that month, "George Washington, Esquire, General and Commander in Chief of the Forces of the United States of America" issued a printed proclamation:

"By virtue of the Power and Direction to Me especially given, I hereby enjoin and require all Persons residing within seventy Miles of my Head Quarters to thresh one Half of their Grain by the 1st Day of February, and the other Half by the 1st Day of March next ensuing, on Pain, in case of Failure, of having all that shall remain in Sheaves after the Period above mentioned, seized by the Commissaries and Quarter-Masters of the Army, and paid for as Straw."

Hearts of farmers must have sunk when they read that proclamation. For they knew that obedience meant they must sell their grain to the army—and be paid in nearly worthless Continental currency.

A Substitute for Shoes

Foot gear—scarce even at the beginning of hostilities—became an ever-increasing problem for Washington and his forces. Shoes of the era were simply made on a straight last, so that it made no difference whether a shoe was put on one's right foot or left. But the supply of cobblers and of finished leather was limited. Earlier, great quantities of shoes had been imported from England.

Under combat conditions, boots took a dreadful beating. They often became water soaked, then were allowed to dry so quickly that they cracked and split. Soldiers tried to ease the aches of their feet by wrapping them with cloth—but especially during long marches the wrappings were prone to deteriorate and become so full of holes that they were worse than useless.

By the winter of 1777, the problem of shoes for the Contintental Army had long passed the crisis stage. Months earlier, a Connecticut military surgeon had jotted down a poignant description of the typical foot soldier: "his bare feet are seen thro' his worn-out shoes, his legs nearly naked from the tattered remains of an only pair of stockings, his Breeches not sufficient to cover his nakedness. His whole appearance pictures a person forsaken & discouraged. He crys, 'I am Sick, my feet lame, my legs are sore, my body is covered with tormenting Itch.'"

Men could survive and fight with tattered breeches. But winter marches without footwear seemed impossible. Remembering the moccasins he had seen during his early military campaigns, George Washington himself offered a reward of ten dollars in gold to the person who would devise "a substitute for shoes, made of raw hides." The reward was never paid—because the hides were not available. Washington's men wrapped their feet in rags, but often left trails of blood in the snow when they marched.

A Coat of Blue Manchester Velvet

During his long stay as a diplomatic emissary in Paris, Benjamin Franklin was widely feted as a sort of homespun philosopher. In keeping with this role, he dressed in the simplest fashion: plain clothing without ornaments and a fur cap. To complete the picture he often carried a long cane of apple wood, though he did not need it for walking.

Franklin's colleagues, Silas Deane and Arthur Lee, found it hard to conceal their astonishment when the Sage of Philadelphia appeared on the evening of Friday, February 6, 1778, wearing an expensive coat made of figured blue Manchester velvet.

Franklin enjoyed their astonishment for a time. Then he explained that he had owned the coat for years. He was, in fact, wearing it when he appeared before a committee of the English Parliament in 1774—only to be violently and rudely attacked by Alexander Wedderburn for his role in making public inflammatory correspondence from the pen of Massachusetts Governor Thomas Hutchinson.

It was one of the most humiliating experiences of his life, the American told his colleagues. Smarting under insults he could not answer without making matters worse, he had retired from service the expensive coat prepared especially for the occasion.

Carefully saved, the coat of blue Manchester velvet was due that very evening to "get a little revenge," he explained. Wearing it and looking not at all like the Benjamin Franklin familiar through paintings and engravings, the printer-philosopher-diplomat made his way to the Hotel de Lautrec. There he signed the Treaty of Alliance between the U. S. and France—the most important single diplomatic coup of the war for rebels against the authority of England.

Several Thousand Tomahawks

Suffering of Washington and his men at Valley Forge was due to many factors. Some of them, such as the severe winter and the depreciation of Continental currency, are generally familiar. Not so well known is the fact that part of the plight of the patriots stemmed from British success in seizing weapons and supplies at every opportunity.

One of the larger hauls came from a supply depot near the Schuylkill River itself. Acting under orders from Howe, a party of British raiders blundered upon what was—for the era—an enormous cache.

According to the official report listing the materials seized, in a single day the Continentals lost—through carelessness in leaving their supplies unguarded—a great variety of items:

> 3,800 Barrels of Flour, Soap, and candles
> 25 Barrels of Horse Shoes
> Several thousand Tomahawks
> Kettles and Intrenching Tools
> 20 Hogsheads of Resin

No one knows precisely why the tomahawks were there. Nothing in the entire saga of the conflict suggests that Washington ever became so short of weapons that he seriously considered providing some of his troops with tomahawks.

Loss of these weapons therefore created no major problem. But in the case of the goods that were stored with them it was another story. Hundreds of horses went unshod because there were not enough shoes for animals whose masters were themselves sometimes barefoot; flour, soap, candles, and resin were as vital to the war as gunpowder and lead.

Unseasonably Early Shad

Spring, 1778, found Washington's forces at Valley Forge desperately near the point of actual starvation. Though all available civilian supplies for miles around had been seized, there was not nearly enough food to put men into condition for fighting likely to begin as soon as the weather became favorable.

In this emergency, a squadron of soldiers who happened to be passing along the banks of the Schuylkill River heard strange noises and saw sights new to most of them. There was a subdued but unbroken humming in the air. Meanwhile, the surface of the river was riffled in a fashion that no wind had ever been seen to cause. Here and there, the water was briefly cut by thin black things that looked for all the world like knife blades.

"Shad!" shouted a native of the region. "The shad are running early! God . . . how many of them there are!"

Hastily summoned soldiers jumped into the river with whatever implements they could find: rakes, shovels, pitchforks, and even branches broken from trees. Major Henry Lee, who feared that the fish would escape upstream, ordered horsemen to ride into the river and form a living barrier.

Many Continental soldiers recorded in their diaries the providential run of shad, much earlier than could have been expected. No one bothered to make an accurate inventory. But so long as the fish stayed fresh, every man had plenty with which to fill his stomach. Tons and tons of those early shad were salted and dried over campfires, providing part of the food that was to enable Washington's men to take the offensive once more.

A Day of Jubilation

Because it is linked with adoption of the Declaration of Independence, present-day Americans celebrate July 4 in especially boisterous ways. But in the nation's early years, May 6, 1778, was a day of jubilation that far exceeded July 4, 1776.

Under the leadership of Silas Deane, American commissioners worked out with France a Treaty of Alliance (plus a treaty of amity and commerce) on February 6, 1778. It didn't have official standing in the world community of nations, though, until ratified by the Continental Congress.

A messenger reached York, Pennsylvania on May 2, bearing a copy of the history-making document. Congress made ratification formal on May 4. Swift couriers took word of the matter to Washington, who considered the occasion important enough to warrant a special set of orders. Penned on May 5, the communique from the commander in chief to all officers and men in the Continental Army established May 6 as a day of jubilation:

"It having pleased the Almighty Ruler of the Universe propitiously to defend the cause of the United States of America and finally by raising us up a powerful friend, among the Princes of the Earth, to Establish Our Liberty and Independence upon lasting foundations; It becomes us to set apart a day, for fully acknowledging the Divine Goodness, and celebrating the important event, which we owe to his Benign interposition," Washington said.

His judgment of the issue was right. Viewed from the perspective of two hundred years, there is little doubt that the American cause would have been lost had not France rushed to the aid of the colonies—done largely in order to weaken the hand of her old enemy, Britain.

The Mischianza

Officers under the command of General Sir William Howe, head of British forces that occupied Philadelphia during the spring of 1778, conceived the idea of giving a banquet in honor of their chief. The idea snowballed, and before it came to a stopping point it had produced the most extravagant event of its type in eighteenth-century America.

Held at Walnut Grove, the estate of the wealthy Wharton family, it was from the start designed to be by invitation only. One London-based firm is said to have sold £12,000 worth of silks, laces, and other costly materials for which the belles of Philadelphia vied.

Just 750 invitations were issued for the entertainment—which started at 4:00 P.M. on May 18 and lasted for twelve hours.

For most who attended it, the Mischianza was remembered for the rest of their lives. Memories of it therefore made a natural subject of letters exchanged between two persons who had played important roles in the festival. One of them was Major John André, who with Captain Oliver Delancey was in charge of making plans. The other was lovely young Margaret (Peggy) Shippen, ambitious daughter of a prominent Philadelphia leader.

Only a few weeks after Peggy became Mrs. Benedict Arnold she was writing about the Mischianza and other memories to Major André—using the correspondence as a cover for the exchange of earliest overtures between her husband and André, eventually leading to Arnold's treason.

Sam Smedley, Privateer

Some accounts of the Revolution incorrectly credit Samuel Smedley with having been the nation's youngest naval commander at age fifteen. Born in 1753, he did go to sea at age fifteen, but he was no longer an adolescent when hostilities broke out. His career was typical of many privateers, most of whom are all but forgotten.

In 1777 Smedley (by now a first lieutenant and hence commanding officer of his vessel) personally supervised rebuilding of the brig *Defence*. He had the ship lengthened by eighteen feet, giving her an overall length of eighty-nine feet. In spite of her twenty-five foot beam, the ship drew only eight feet of water. She was armed with a battery of sixteen six pounders brought from Boston to the shipyard at Salisbury, Connecticut, by an oxteam.

Though lightly armed, the ship was so maneuverable that she easily outsailed most British vessels of the era. On a single cruise that began in June, 1778, Smedley and his men "fell in with three British privateers, catpured two of them—these captures producing upwards of $80,000 alone."

Twice taken prisoner, Smedley was responsible for the capture of at least fourteen British vessels. Prize money he received from his captures made him a comparatively wealthy man.

Smedley sailed under the flag of Connecticut and was never a member of the fledgling Continental Navy. His career vividly illustrates the dilemma that American leaders faced. A good man could make more money from prizes in a month than he could get from five years' wages as a sailor. Therefore most American naval action of the war was by privateers, not vessels of the Continental Navy.

"A Most Auspicious Omen"

Kaskaskia, located at the mouth of the river for which it was named and lying about fifty miles south of St. Louis, was generally considered a pivotal fortress. If it could be taken, the entire Illinois country—including regions that now make up Illinois, Indiana, and Ohio—might be claimed in the name of the United States. Besides striking a blow to Britain, such a move would open up the possibility of increasing contact and trade with friendly Spanish leaders.

Frontiersman George Rogers Clark managed to persuade Thomas Jefferson that the feat could be pulled off. Jefferson, in turn, induced Governor Patrick Henry to get the Burgesses of Virginia to appropriate £1,200 for Clark's proposed mission.

Clark assembled a force of two hundred men at a point just south of present-day Lousiville, Kentucky. Their first dangerous step involved shooting the rapids of the Ohio River only hours after embarking on June 26, 1778. Even veteran woodsmen wanted to turn back when they saw that the sun was going into eclipse. It was a bad omen, they insisted.

"Not so," protested their leader. "If the eclipse is total, it will prove to be a most auspicious omen, indeed." No one knows whether or not Clark had advance knowledge that the eclipse would indeed be total. But his confident words persuaded his men that darkening of the sun meant that the fires of Britain would be put out—so his handful of frontiersmen followed him to victory after staggering victory. No other U. S. military expedition by so small a force has added so vast a territory to the nation.

Thayendanegea

By 1778, the noted Mohawk leader Thayendanegea was well known to most patriots in the northeastern U.S.— if not to their descendants.

Reared among white men and sometimes known as Joseph Brant or Joseph Brandt, Thayendanegea had for six years helped to run the Indian Department administered by the British out of Quebec. On the outbreak of armed hostilities between colonists and the mother country, Thayendanegea had immediately offered his services to the British.

Tradition holds that the chieftain promised each of his warriors an opportunity "to feast on a Bostonian and to drink his blood." General Sir Guy Carlton, commanding officer of forces in Canada, wanted nothing to do with butchery. He agreed only to employ a party of forty or fifty men as scouts. Colonel Daniel Claus, who was present at negotiations between British and Mohawks, reported that "the Indians were somewhat disgusted at their offer being rejected."

Later, though Thayendanegea had plenty of opportunity for action. Leading a force of approximately 1,000 braves he fought at Fort Stanwix, New York, in 1777, and saw his forces take a terrible beating. An opportunity for revenge presented itself the following August. Thayendanegea and his men swooped upon the frontier settlement of Cherry Valley in the Wyoming Valley of Pennsylvania and wiped it out. Even women and children were taken prisoner or killed.

From that time, frontiersmen regarded Thayendanegea with execration. But because he was the most influential of living Indians, after the wars were over he went to Philadelphia for a meeting with George Washington. He claimed to have received 1,000 guineas as down payment, plus offer of an ultimate reward of £20,000 for arranging "a peace with the Ohio Indians." No other native American profited so greatly from the Revolution.

Good Intentions but a Comic-Opera Performance

Once a treaty of military alliance had been signed by American envoys and French diplomats, secret support of colonial forces by France ceased. England's old enemy came out in the open, boldly sent a fleet to North America to help tip the scales against the king of England.

Charles Theodat, Comte D'Estaing, was the admiral in charge of this fleet. He arrived in America waters in July, 1778, and remained for fifteen months.

A letter written on October 28, aboard the French warship *Languedoc*, is evidence of his sincerity and zeal. Addressed to "all of the Ancient French in North America," it was prepared for circulation in Canada. D'Estaing recalled old quarrels in his emotion-charged appeal for Canadians to come to the aid of colonial forces fighting their own old enemy.

"Can the Canadians, who saw the brave Montcalm fall in their defense, can they become the enemies of his nephews?" D'Estaing asked. "Can they fight against their former leaders, and arm themselves against their kinsmen? At the bare mention of their names, the weapons would fall out of their hands."

In spite of his good intentions, actions of the French admiral constituted a comic-opera performance. Even his letter to Canadians had no noticeable impact.

Though he commanded a large fleet, heavily armed and manned by experienced sailors, he didn't win a single engagement. At Chesapeake Bay, he arrived too late to bottle up the British fleet. He failed to attack in New York and again at Newport, Rhode Island. He planned a futile assault on Newfoundland and wasted months getting ready for it. Then he was chief strategist in the Battle of Savannah, in which French and American forces were badly beaten.

Aware that D'Estaing was a liability rather than an asset, American leaders were forced to tolerate him for fear of offending their ally, France.

Bourbon County, Kentucky

More than any other European ruler outside the British isles, King Louis XVI of France was vitally interested in the course of events in North America. As a result of the Seven Years' War, France had suffered a crushing defeat by England and was eager for revenge. An overwhelming victory by Continental Forces under George Washington would have repercussions across the Atlantic by "redressing the balance of the Old World."

Encouraged by his foreign ministers, Louis XVI put substantial sums of money on the line to aid American rebels in secret. Then the whole climate of Europe changed suddenly in the aftermath of the battle of Saratoga. England began putting out peace feelers, and there were signs that Spain might move to recognize and aid the new nation that was coming into being.

French secrecy ended on January 7, 1778. That day a royal council unanimously endorsed "a treaty of amity and commerce with the United States of America." One month later, on February 6, a formal treaty was signed.

In addition to fostering economic aid to the U.S. the treaty was a powerful psychological weapon. Even in the American backwoods the import was not missed. Settlers in the practically uncharted "wilderness of Kentucky" moved in December, 1778, to let the French ruler know Americans would forever be grateful. They called for the use of Bourbon—the French royal line to which Louis XVI belonged—as the name for a huge "county" that was not even marked on maps of the era.

Later subdivided several times, Bourbon County became famous as the native home of a distinctively American type of whisky—which took the name of the region named in gratitude to the Bourbon ruler of France.

A Female Guerrilla

Unlike the handful of women who fought with their husbands or in disguise on battlefields, female patriots who resisted behind the lines got little or no attention. One of them, Nancy Hart, was probably typical of many whose names have been lost to history. Her exploits were not reported in print until half a century after hostilities had ceased.

Born somewhere on the Pennsylvania or the North Carolina frontier about 1735, Ann Morgan grew up in rough-and-tumble country. Like many women of the era, she could hunt and shoot as well as most men. Her cabin was decorated with trophies —bearskins and antlers—to prove her marksmanship.

British forces moved to the Savannah River in December, 1778. Among the cities they occupied was Augusta, Georgia —not far from where the former Miss Morgan (long known as Nancy) lived with her husband, prosperous plantation owner Benjamin Hart.

When patriot forces needed intelligence about British activities in Augusta, Nancy disguised herself as a man and in early January entered the occupied city. She posed as "touched," or crazy, successfully crossed back through British lines with details of activities in the city.

A few months later, six Tories descended upon her cabin to quiz her about her doings. She sent her daughter to blow a conch shell to call the men folks to her help—but by the time they got there, Nancy had disarmed the six men and was holding them prisoners. At the woman's insistence, the six were hanged from nearby pine trees.

Hundreds—perhaps thousands—of other female guerrilla fighters hampered British operations and helped bring victory to patriots without leaving behind the accounts of their exploits.

"A Joshua in Buckskin"

Vincennes, in the Northwest Territory, remained the last significant British outpost of the region after Major George Rogers
Clark and his men had captured other posts. Initially small,
Clark's contingent of men had been reduced by sickness and by
bullets of the enemy. No fully rational man would have presumed
to attempt the long and arduous march that would pit frontiersmen with rifles against a British fort that mounted twelve heavy
field pieces.

Advancing slowly through desolate water-logged country,
Clark seems to have feared desertion or mutiny more than he
feared British guns. With a company of twenty-five selected
riflemen, Captain Joseph Bowman brought up the rear of the
straggling little "army"—under orders to shoot any man who
tried to slip away from the party.

From a captured Frenchman, Clark learned that British com-
mandant Colonel Henry Hamilton knew nothing about the plan to
take Vincennes and adjacent Fort Sackville, the more important
objective from the military standpoint.

Clark's weary men reached Vincennes late on February 24,
1779. Instead of attempting a surprise attack, he formed his
riflemen into two companies and sent them marching up and
down the streets of the frontier town in order to announce their
presence. British defenders moved into Fort Sackville, confident
that their heavy guns could hold off any number of men with
small arms.

Having boldly announced his arrival, Clark operated like "a
Joshua in Buckskin." He demanded the surrender of the fort, and
when it did not come set his sharpshooters to picking off enemy
gunners one by one. It never was necessary to storm the fortress;
outwitted and bewildered British surrendered—giving U.S.
commissioners a key bargaining position at the time the Treaty of
Paris was signed.

Mrs. Benedict Arnold

Margaret (Peggy) Shippen was high in Philadelphia society. As the daughter of the Chief Justice of Pennsylvania, she had entrance into "the most elegant drawing rooms and the most elaborate ballrooms."

Peggy was good-looking, and she knew it. Friends said that she was as ambitious as she was charming. Her father, a Quaker, protested that "my gay young daughter spends money faster than I can make it."

When Continental troops drove the British out of Philadelphia in June, 1778, Peggy Shippen saw an opportunity to realize some of her ambitions. The patriot in charge of the new troops of occupation was a widower nearly twice Peggy's age—but himself ambitious and susceptible to flattery.

On April 8, 1779, Peggy Shippen became Mrs. Benedict Arnold. Since the bridegroom had a bad leg from a war injury, he leaned on a soldier when standing and propped his leg on a stool when sitting.

Bad leg and all, Arnold had access to General Washington and to confidential dispatches of the Continental Army. Within weeks after he took Peggy Shippen as his bride, he was engaged in the first tentative negotiations that eventually led him to sell out his country.

His wife's role in Arnold's treachery was not fully disclosed until 150 years after her death. In 1941, historian Carl Van Doren published the secret papers of Sir Henry Clinton—and disclosed that Peggy Arnold had helped to code and decode some of her husband's earliest letters to a British officer with whom she was already intimately acquainted. That officer was Major André—later captured and executed as a spy.

Without the beauty, audacity, and ambition of his wife as variables in a complex human equation, Benedict Arnold might have remained loyal to his country.

Blackstone's *Commentaries on the Laws of England*

English jurist Sir William Blackstone (1723-1780) dropped out of active legal practice to begin lecturing on the laws of England when he was just thirty years old. Eventually his *Commentaries* became a standard reference source throughout the English-speaking world; today, attorneys usually refer to the four books as simply "Blackstone."

His first volume, published hastily in November, 1765, included many errors. Still it was an overnight sensation. New editions were rushed through the press in the decade that followed.

It was the fifth Oxford edition of Blackstone's *Commentaries* to which Major John André and General Benedict Arnold turned when they sought a source of a code that couldn't be broken. Each word in code messages that they exchanged included three numbers: page, line, and word. Both men had identical copies of Blackstone from which to work.

Using the already-famous legal commentary in a fashion that would have astonished its author, the two men exchanged numerous detailed code letters as Arnold bargained for the money and rank he wanted in return for a sell-out.

Writing to André on May 23, 1779, General Arnold used Blackstone to encode a letter saying that proposals originated by Sir Henry Clinton were agreeable to him. He provided the British with military intelligence—perhaps as a token of good faith —then came back to his original theme.

"I will cooperate when an opportunity offers," he promised (in code), "and as life and every thing is at stake I will expect some certainty, my property here secure and a revenue equivalent to the risk and service done." Turning to his own trusty copy of Blackstone's *Commentaries*, André decoded the letter of acceptance and transmitted it to his superiors.

A Leaky Old East India Ship

Commanding the Continental Navy vessel *Ranger*, John Paul Jones took the war to England in the spring of 1778. He struck at Whitehaven on the northwest coast, tried but did not succeed in destroying ships lying there. But the fact that the American rebels could make the war felt in the homeland was a source of consternation to the British.

Americans and their French allies rejoiced, however. High-ranking officials of the French government consulted with the American commissioners about the possibility of invading England. John Paul Jones could lead the naval forces, it was suggested, while Lafayette could be put in charge of troops. Liverpool would make a logical target.

Though this idea was eventually scrapped, it gave impetus to French moves aimed at strengthening the Continental Navy.

Jones' *Ranger*, which actually operated as a privateer, had been built in New England and was lightly armed: just eighteen six-pound cannon and six swivels. Pierced for twenty guns, the little ship sailed before the last two could be secured and mounted.

Feted in France as a hero, Jones intimated that he could do a much better job if he had a larger and more heavily armed ship. Government agents assented to this plea, and in response to it got him another. It proved to be the *Duras*—capable of mounting forty guns, but worn out and leaking from long service in trade to the Indies.

Jones accepted the battered old merchantman, transformed it into a warship and named it *Bonhomme Richard* in honor of Benjamin Franklin. When plans for invasion of England were scrapped, he sailed in his new flagship from the port of L'Orient on August 14, 1779. It was the one-time East Indiaman that met the *Serapis* on September 23, and after three hours of bloody fighting gave the Continental Navy one of its most memorable victories.

135

Total War—Against the Six Nations

British use of American Indians—plus independent forays by bands of warriors—created a near panic among frontiersmen in 1778. Particularly devastating raids in Pennsylvania and New York made it clear that the infant United States must reckon not only with Great Britain but also with the Six Nations of the American Indians.

Lands held by these tribesmen extended all the way from Lake Ontario to the Susquehanna River. Contrary to stereotype concepts, they did not live in wigwams and were "primitive" only in the sense that they had not learned the art of metallurgy before the white man came.

Their towns—many of which had stood for hundreds of years—included dozens or even scores of buildings. Some of them, built of stone, were equipped with glazed windows. Fine orchards, carefully tended for generation after generation, showed that these people were not the wandering warriors, living off the land, who are usually depicted in art and fiction.

George Washington himself drew up final plans for action against the Six Nations, ordered "total destruction of their settlements." To accomplish this objective, big forces of men under General James Clinton and General John Sullivan moved into Indian territory late in the summer of 1779.

Sullivan was first to strike. On August 29 his men reached the town of Chemung with "between 30 & 40 Houses, plus a Chapel and Council House." The town was levelled to the ground; crops were burned; orchards were destroyed. Systematic destruction continued for about two months—during which period the oldest and most stable American Indian towns east of the Mississippi River were captured and pillaged by men fighting to win their own freedom from England's rule.

Cannon Harmless at Point-Blank Range

John Paul Jones' exclamation, "I have not yet begun to fight!" is one of the most famous sentences of the Revolution. Most Americans are at least vaguely aware that he made it when facing apparent defeat by an English foe. But the circumstances under which Jones' boast proved a prelude to victory have few if any parallels in the history of naval warfare.

The British man-o'-war *Serapis* mounted forty-four guns. These made her—on paper—approximately an even match for Jones' *Bonhomme Richard*. But the American vessel was old, having been converted after long service as a merchantman. Her big guns had not been carefully tested. Two of them—both eighteen-pounders—exploded when fired. Numerous members of the crew were killed, an entire section of deck was wrecked, and no one dared to fire the vessel's other big guns.

Rigging of the *Serapis* became tangled in the bowsprit of the American vessel so that it was impossible to disengage the ships even had both commanders wanted to do so. It was in this situation that Captain Pearson of the *Serapis* asked if Jones wished to surrender, and the American gave his immortal reply.

Locked together, the two ships continued to pour fire toward one another. By all logic, the *Bonhomme Richard* should have proved to be a sitting duck. But logic didn't prevail. Earlier explosions had torn big holes in the ship—and from point-blank range the heavy balls from cannon of the *Serapis* passed harmlessly through those holes. At any other distance, the fire would have been lethal. Absolutely ineffective under the circumstances, it did little additional damage to the crippled American vessel—whose men poured heavy fire on decks of the *Serapis* and had to abandon their own ship almost immediately after the *Serapis* surrendered.

"Tarleton's Quarter"

Since medieval times it had been customary for victors in battle to show mercy to foes who cried "Quarter! Quarter!" and offered to surrender without resistance. But the battle of Waxhaws, North Carolina, in May, 1780, did not conform to the rules of chivalry. Colonel Banastre Tarleton, commanding officer of a troop formed chiefly from American-born loyalists, ignored the white flag when patriots displayed it.

Tarleton's dragoons used their bayonets to slaughter men who had already thrown down their weapons. Whether deliberately planned or a spontaneous fruit of concerted action by undisciplined victors, the massacre was one of the bloodiest of the war. Light-Horse Harry Lee said of it, "This bloody day only wanted the war dance and the roasting fire to have placed it first in the records of torture and death in the West."

Following the day of slaughter in May, 1780, patriots of the region adopted "Tarleton's Quarter!" as a battle cry to signify that even when a redcoat or Tory offered to surrender, he would not be allowed to live. Most killing done in revenge for brutality at Waxhaws was on a sporadic basis.

But following their victory at King's Mountain, adjacent to the North Carolina line, patriots applied "Tarleton's Quarter" with a vengeance. Dozens of prisoners were shot after they had formally surrendered; one group of nine prisoners was hanged (three at a time) from a huge oak tree. No general officer on either side sanctioned such tactics; in most battles, any man who threw down his arms was guaranteed relative safety in a prison camp, where he could hope to be exchanged within a few months.

London Tower

Famous as a royal fortress, royal residence, prison, and place of execution for high-born Englishmen, London Tower played host to an American for nearly fourteen months.

Henry Laurens, leading merchant of Charleston, South Carolina, and for a time the President of the Continental Congress, was in 1779 picked by Americans to try to negotiate a commercial agreement with Holland. In pursuit of his mission Laurens sailed from Philadelphia in August, 1780, on the brig *Mercury*. Hailed by men of the British frigate *Vestal* in waters off Newfoundland, the *Mercury* hove to, and Laurens hastily dumped his diplomatic pouch into the sea.

Retrieved by watchful British tars, the papers were later used as a pretext for British declaration of war upon the Dutch. Meanwhile, although he was on a peaceful commercial mission, Laurens was detained "on suspicion of high treason." Taken to England as a prisoner, he spent a brief period in Dartmouth jail. After lengthy examination by high officials, the American was told his fate by Mr. Chamberlain, Solicitor of the Treasury.

"Mr. Laurens," he said, according to the merchant's own narrative, "you are to be sent to the Tower of London, not to a prison; you must have no idea of a prison."

In the history-soaked Tower where members of British royalty had been imprisoned and executed, the American was given about twenty square feet of space with a warder for his constant companion and a fixed bayonet under his window. Captors charged him rent, board, and even the wages of his warders. On the last day of December, 1781, he was released on heavy bail; four months later he was exchanged for Lord Cornwallis—who had fallen into American hands after the disaster of Yorktown.

Foiled by the *Vulture*

The British sloop of war *Vulture* was too small and too lightly armed to play a major role in a naval engagement. Yet this little vessel played a crucial role in disrupting the plans of Benedict Arnold and may have been responsible for the fact that his plot to betray his country was unsuccessful.

Arnold and Major André, his British contact man, had completed all of their bargaining. Terms under which Arnold was to defect to the British, selling out his countrymen by delivering vital plans of the fortifications at West Point and of coming military movements on the part of Continental forces, had been fixed. All that remained was to execute the plan.

Its terms called for Arnold's delivering of papers to André, after which the British major was to board the *Vulture*. Then stationed in the Hudson River near West Point, it would be easy for the vessel to transport André—and the papers—to British headquarters in New York. Or Arnold could go overland to Dobbs Ferry, meet André there, and proceed with him.

Probably with the idea of making sure that all preparations aboard the ship had been completed, Arnold himself had eight oarsmen row him toward the *Vulture* in a barge. That was on the morning of September 11, 1780. Everything should have moved like clockwork, and probably would have, had Arnold not forgotten to fasten a flag of truce to his barge.

That omission caused men of the *Vulture* to fire upon Arnold and make him retreat to a tree-covered bluff. The traitor was almost killed, and the time-table of his operation was hopelessly disrupted. Consequently André was captured on September 20, and Arnold's role was known to Washington almost at once. Had guns of the *Vulture* not fired history might have been different.

Major Ferguson's Defiance

Patrick Ferguson, a soldier since early adolescence, prided himself on his knowledge of guns. The breech-loading rifle he invented was the only such weapon used by the British in the Revolution. It used a pointed bullet and could be fired five or six times a minute; only about two thousand of these rifles ever got into service.

The soldier-inventor arrived in the colonies in 1777, fought bravely and well at Brandywine, Charleston, and other points. His special competence persuaded Lord Cornwallis that Ferguson was just the man to recruit and lead a special corps of American-born loyalists and fugitives from justice. A band such as this would be ideal, Cornwallis reasoned, for plundering the American countryside.

Ferguson drummed up recruits and for a time was the terror of the Carolinas. With his force nearly doubled by a contingent of British regulars, he moved toward the North Carolina border. Mountain men in the Watauga settlement of what is now Tennessee received word from the Scottish warrior that they must "declare for the Crown or prepare to be invaded and exterminated."

Instead of running, the backwoodsmen took the offensive. Ferguson led his men to the top of a narrow stony ride on King's Mountain, dug in and noted in his diary that he "defied God Almighty and all the rebels out of Hell" to storm this high ground.

Unaware of the professional soldier's defiant stand, mountain men attacked from two sides simultaneously, then completely enveloped Ferguson's band. Ferguson himself was killed along with about four hundred of his men (many of whom were shot after having surrendered). An additional seven hundred Tories were taken prisoner—and only eighty eight patriots were killed or wounded. Raw courage of inexperienced men more than made up for strategic advantages of location and years of experience on the battlefield.

Henry Dawkins, Master Engraver

Because currency issued by the Continental Congress was hastily produced on whatever paper was available, it took little skill to make counterfeits that easily passed in trade. Most spurious bills of this sort were printed even more poorly than the genuine ones they imitated. In New York City, however, merchants and bankers became aware that "very superior counterfeits" were in circulation during the spring of 1776.

George Washington himself took a hand in trying to catch the culprit—for the economy of the new nation was endangered. Under his orders, a military raiding party surrounded a house on Long Island and seized printing presses, counterfeit Continental currency, and an engraver named Henry Dawkins.

Dawkins learned to engrave upon metals in London and came to the New World about 1753. He was among the earliest engravers to work on copper in America. Consequently the bills produced under his supervision were far superior to ordinary counterfeit notes. After his arrest in May, 1776, some evidence was brought forward suggesting that he was in the pay of British agents who were trying to undermine the strength of the currency issued by patriots. This charge was never proved, however.

Regardless of whether Dawkins was a secret agent or merely a counterfeiter out for easy money, he petitioned the New York Committee of Safety in October, 1776, "for a termination of his sorrows by a death." Apparently he won his release—and entered the services of the patriots.

On October 13, 1780, *Journals of the Continental Congress* recorded payment to Henry Dawkins of $1500 "on account for engraving and altering the border and back pieces for striking the bills of credit of the U.S." Few if any other counterfeiters have entered the service of any government; Dawkins, who is in a class by himself, dropped out of sight after 1780.

George Washington Masterminds a Kidnapping

In public, George Washington showed few signs of emotion when he learned that his fellow officer Benedict Arnold had deserted to the British. Privately, he was furious. Arnold's treason must not—could not—go unpunished, he said.

Intelligence reports made it clear that the traitor had reached New York. Far beyond the reach of patriot troops, he was engaged in raising a corps of men—to be led by himself—to fight against his former comrade in arms.

In this situation, Washington masterminded what was perhaps the most bizarre plot of the entire Revolution. Since he couldn't seize Arnold by force of arms, he would arrange to kidnap the traitor and have him spirited to American lines for arrest, conviction, and execution. At least, that is what Washington hoped and expected.

The commander in chief enlisted the aid of Major Henry Lee, an old hand at espionage. Lee listened, agreed that it would indeed be possible to kidnap Benedict Arnold inside British lines and bring him to justice. For the job he recommended twenty-four-year-old Sergeant John Champe of Loudoun County, Virginia.

On the night of October 20, 1780, Champe pretended to desert his unit. Actually acting under orders from Washington, he got across the Hudson River and reached a British gunboat—still wearing his Light Horse uniform. He offered to join the British cause and got passage to New York, where he managed to enlist in Benedict Arnold's corps. By December 11, the plan to kidnap Arnold was complete; with the aid of another undercover agent Champe would seize him and rush him to waiting patriots in New Jersey.

Fate then took a hand. Just twenty-four hours before Washington's kidnapping plot was to have been executed Arnold ordered his men—including John Champe—to embark on transports for a voyage to Virginia, thereby foiling the plot.

Loyalty Above Personal Feelings

Especially in the southeast, where his troops fought some of their bloodiest battles, Lord Cornwallis is still a symbol of English oppression.

His fierce loyalty to duty and devotion to the king were vividly demonstrated in January, 1781. After the Battle of Cowpens, S.C., Cornwallis decided to pursue defeated Americans as they fled northward. Since his foes were accustomed to the country and were less heavily encumbered than were his own forces, the British general knew he had no hope of catching up with them without taking drastic action. So he ordered his men to burn everything not absolutely essential to rapid march of unknown duration.

His forces were camped at Ramsour's Mill, about twenty miles southwest of the Catawba River. For two days the British sorted gear, burned tents, baggage, extra clothing, and even supplies. They saved a few of their sturdiest wagons, consigned the rest to the flames.

It was this do or die action on the part of Cornwallis that enabled him to move into Virginia—planning to unite with British forces in New York in order to have a force that no American commander could stop.

Strangely, the general who burned baggage and supplies so that he could hurry after rebels was actually sympathetic to the American cause. In 1766 he had publicly demonstrated that view by becoming one of only four English peers who supported Lord Camden in his opposition to the parliamentary resolution that asserted the right of taxation in America. Yet Lord Cornwallis put loyalty above his personal feelings—and King George III knew it. Sent to America as a major general in the very year he had opposed taxation of America, he never wavered in his loyalty—but the irony of war made his defeat at Yorktown the capstone to rebel victory.

"A Genuine Penitence"

During the fearful winter of 1780-81, Continental troops often went for days without proper food and for months without pay. Additional grievances centered in the shortage of warm clothing, and in disagreements about terms of enlistment.

These factors led to outright mutiny, with violence flaring on the first day of the new year. Pennsylvania troops stationed at Morristown, New Jersey, killed or wounded several officers. Then they started toward Philadelphia to demand that Congress respond to their grievances.

Two weeks earlier, a formal report by General Anthony Wayne to President Joseph Reed of the Pennsylvania Supreme Executive Council had detailed the suffering and grievances of the men. No action was taken in response to Wayne's plea because authorities had no resources with which to respond.

But when mutiny flared, George Washington acted quickly. In one of the least-known incidents of the war, the commander in chief quashed the mutiny—then forced mutineers to execute three of their own leaders.

One of Washington's own accounts of the affair, included in a letter to the Commission for Redressing the Grievances of the New Jersey Line, was written at Ringwood on January 27.

"I detached a body of troops under Major Genl.[Robert] Howe with orders to compel the mutineers to unconditional submission and execute on the spot a few of the principal incendiaries," he reported.

"This has been effected this morning; and we have reason to believe the mutinous disposition of the troops is now completely subdued and succeeded by a genuine penitence."

Governor Jefferson Under Attack

Many leaders, both British and American, felt that Virginia was the key to the war. If the commonwealth could be seized, Cornwallis said repeatedly in councils of war, the conflict would be over. Through intelligence reports this view was well known to Continental leaders.

Governor Thomas Jefferson appealed to Washington for help, but was rebuffed. Writing from headquarters at Ramapo, New Jersey, on June 29, 1780, the commander in chief told the Virginia governor that "our situation in this quarter precludes every hope of affording you further assistance." Washington cited "short inlistments, delays in filling up our battalions, and the great deficiency in military stores." All these factors reduced his own forces, he said, "to a mere handful of men left as it were at the mercy of a formidable enemy."

Virginia would have to help herself.

In this critical situation, Jefferson the statesman and orator proved strangely lethargic as an administrator. He mustered a few hundred militiamen, poorly trained, and assigned the defense of Richmond to them. Against this force were pitted trained British troops under the leadership of the arch traitor, Benedict Arnold. Arnold sailed up the James River to a point about twenty-five miles from the capital, then entered it without opposition. Jefferson's defending forces didn't fire a single shot before they fled on January 5, 1781.

So much criticism followed that the great Thomas Jefferson "resigned" as governor—literally vacating the chair without a successor having been named. Later the legislature called for a formal investigation of his administration. Though he was never formally censured, the author of the Declaration of Independence never fully got over the personal injury. Since Jefferson laid much of the blame for the charges against him on the shoulders of Patrick Henry, the two men became permanently estranged.

John Hanson, "Our First President"

George Washington, insist members of the John Hanson Society of Oxon Hill, Maryland, was a Johnny-come-lately who ought to vacate the place of "first in peace, first in war, first in the hearts of his countrymen" to the Swede who rightly deserves it.

Honored on a 1972 U.S. postal card that depicted two notable patriots, Paul Revere and John Hanson, the latter didn't surge into prominence until 1926. Partly to placate Swedish-American constituents, Calvin Coolidge that year described Hanson as "our first president."

That remark won a place (for the first time) for Hanson in the *Encyclopaedia Britannica;* there was no mention of him in the *Encyclopedia Americana* until 1942.

"Our First President" wasn't even a delegate to the First Continental Congress, which met in Philadelphia on September 5, 1774. But the following May he was on hand with proper credentials when the Second Continental Congress met and held his seat throughout the Revolution.

Delegates to the Second Continental Congress couldn't levy taxes. They had no authority to issue money. It was beyond their power to pass laws that would be binding in all thirteen colonies. But they could— and did—elect a presiding officer whom they naturally called the President of the Continental Congress. Peyton Randolph of Virginia was first to hold the office. Under clumsy rules that required rotation of the presidency, John Hanson got the job when Thomas McKean voluntarily gave it up.

So Hanson was first to preside after adoption of the loosely drawn Articles of Confederation (March 1, 1781). It's on that basis that his admirers single him out from the thirteen presiding officers of the Continental Congress and call him our first President.

Rochambeau Signs Articles of Capitulation

Yorktown—the engagement that for practical purposes ended the war—was a major tactical victory for George Washington. But few Americans pay adequate tribute to the French officer who played so large a role in the struggle and who was a signer of the Articles of Capitulation.

Perhaps the ablest general officer in the entire French military establishment, the Comte de Rochambeau reached the theater of war comparatively late—in 1780. He brought with him only four infantry regiments. But the seasoned veterans were the pick of the French army. Far more important, Rochambeau himself was a seasoned strategist who argued strongly for moves he espoused.

By May, 1781, Washington had thrown his personal weight on the side of an expedition aimed at recapturing New York from the British. Rochambeau entered his "strongest objections" to the proposed plans, insisting instead that the army of Cornwallis was much more vulnerable than were forces long entrenched in New York.

During a period of at least ninety days, the French nobleman persisted in his plea that Cornwallis be made the main target. His forces, along with those of Washington, began the long southward march on August 19; five weeks later they joined Lafayette at Williamsburg, Virginia. Rochambeau had known since May that the Comte de Grasse was under orders to bring his strong fleet up the Atlantic coast during the hurricane period in the West Indies. Timing was all-important, he urged; if de Grasse sailed back south before the British surrendered, it would be impossible to block their escape to New York.

Significantly, it was Rochambeau (along with the Comte de Barras) who acted for France in signing Cornwallis' Articles of Capitulation. Virtually unknown by comparison with Lafayette, his countryman gave vital leadership in what became the most vital single campaign of the entire conflict.

Simsbury Mines

Most colonies at some period, and some colonies for extended periods, maintained special prisons for captured loyalists. Little was known about the Simsbury Mines until Ebenezer Hathaway and Thomas Smith led an escape from them in May, 1781.

When trouble between patriots and loyalists began to be seen as inevitable, a Connecticut committee of safety saw a potential use for a cluster of abandoned copper mines at Simsbury (now East Granby). Meager records of the era indicate that the mines were transformed into a prison as early as 1773, though there are no indications of what persons were put into them at that time.

Cells were approximately forty yards below the surface of the ground. According to one contemporary description, "the prisoners are let down by a windlass into the dismal cavern, through a hole, which answers the purposes of conveying their food and air."

Because the Simsbury Mines—now compared with Andersonville of Civil War fame—were considered escape-proof, the caverns played host to a number of celebrated prisoners. Among them were David Mathews, one-time mayor of New York, and William Franklin, noted Tory governor of New Jersey.

Patriots cloaked the foul holes in the ground with secrecy, and it is unlikely that top Revolutionary leaders knew of their existence. Occasional release of a loyalist held there for a time was enough to spread word of the mines among persons who faced the possibility of being sent to them, though. Prisoners, given any choice, preferred almost any other sentence since the Simsbury Mines were regarded as a "Shocking Sentence, Worse Than Death."

James Rivington, Double Agent

London-born James Rivington launched a successful publishing firm in his native city, then decided in 1760 to move to the colonies. He opened bookshops in Philadelphia and in New York became known as the chief North American importer of English books. After extending his chain of stores to Boston, he became owner and publisher of New York's *Royal Gazette*.

It was Rivington's newspaper that became a principal channel for transmission of pro-English news. Much of it was later found to have been manufactured by the editor (who may have acted out of strong loyalty to the crown or may have been in the employ of British authorities).

A long poem on "The American Times" included a bitter attack upon George Washington, with whom Rivington was to have close ties in later years. He used his paper to dramatize problems of patriots and often published accounts with no factual basis. In separate stories, he reported the deaths of both George Washington and Benjamin Franklin. Russian Cossacks were on board a ship headed for North America to help quell the rebellion, he informed his readers after it was generally known in diplomatic sources that Catherine the Great had taken a "hands off" policy toward North America.

Original documents concerning his sudden change of roles in 1781 have long ago disappeared—if they ever existed. For reasons never made clear, the man who had taken George Washington as his favorite journalistic target suddenly switched sides and became a spy for the commander in chief. Because he had been so prominent in loyalist activities, the journalist was able to conceal his new attitude toward Washington (and independence) until he had succeeded in delivering a substantial number of reports to the commander in chief.

Youngest Diplomatic Secretary

John Quincy Adams, eldest son of John and Abigail Adams, got little schooling in his native Massachusetts. Because he went with his father to France at age eleven, he studied there for brief periods. He was not a skilled linguist, but knew far more French than did most American patriots.

This led to Adams' appointment as diplomatic secretary to the U.S. Minister to Russia when the boy was just fourteen.

Francis Dana, named to represent the fledgling nation at the court of Catherine the Great, found himself in trouble almost as soon as he accepted the appointment. French was the official language of the Russian court—and Dana didn't speak or write a word of it.

The diplomat remembered that John Adams' son had spoken French in his presence. He made inquiries, found that John Quincy Adams had studied French in an academy at Passy, near Paris. Moreover he had been a student in the Latin School at Amsterdam for a few months in 1779.

Dana made overtures to his close friend, John Adams, and learned that the boy had entered Leyden University in January, 1781. His father considered him "exceedingly competent for his age" and believed that a term at the Russian court would be worth more to him than the same time spent in the university.

So young Adams left Leyden and set out for St. Petersburg. At age fourteen he became the youngest diplomatic secretary on record and for two years served as the channel through which Francis Dana communicated with Russian officials.

Catherine the Great didn't respond to overtures, though. Pondering the humiliation of the Russian fiasco, Benjamin Franklin observed that "a virgin state should preserve its virgin character, and not go about suitoring for alliances, but wait with decent dignity for the application of others."

Tropical Storms Helped Change the World

Francois Joseph Paul de Grasse, Marquis de Grasse-Tilly, was as French as his name suggests. As commander of a fleet in New World waters he often acted boldly, sometimes almost in whimsical fashion. He didn't care to risk the loss of fine warships temporarily based in Haiti and knew from veterans of those waters that tropical storms can be expected practically every year.

Partly to escape danger from hurricanes, de Grasse ordered his vessels to move northward. Lacking this incentive, there is no reason to believe he would have been in a position to encounter the British fleet commanded by Admiral Thomas Graves.

The French had the numerical advantage—twenty-four ships of the line against nineteen. So the admiral who had sailed away from hurricane-troubled waters decided to close with the British. Both sides suffered heavy losses, with the issue still undecided. Fleets disentangled themselves after the fierce battle of September 5, 1781, and for four days sailed along parallel courses without renewing the battle.

This sequence of events played a vital but often unrecognized part in Washington's spectacular victory at Yorktown. Cornwallis had expected to put his men aboard British vessels and move them swiftly and safely to New York. Only the presence of the French fleet—battered from the September battle but still too formidable to enable Cornwallis to escape by sea—kept British forces bottled up where Washington could push their backs to the wall.

Practically all the glory that stems from British capitulation at Yorktown belongs to Washington, of course. But without de Grasse and the French fleet he couldn't have acted as he did. And had the West Indies not been noted for hurricanes, de Grasse and his warships would have been far away in warm southern waters.

Wanted: Recruits

In spite of some notable victories by Continental forces, the military manpower situation was desperate toward the end of 1781. To foster the flow of recruits, recruiting parties—complete with military bands—spent two to five days at villages and towns.

A poster of the era is addressed "To all Brave, Healthy, Able Bodied, and Well Disposed Young Men . . . Who Have Any Inclination to Join the Troops, Now Raising Under General Washington." Purpose of the recruitment is to secure men "for the defence of the Liberties and Independence of the United States against the hostile designs of foreign enemies."

Upon signing up, each recruit received a bounty of twelve dollars. In addition he was promised "an annual and fully sufficient supply of good and handsome cloathing, a daily allowance of a large and ample ration of provisions, together with SIXTY dollars a year in GOLD and SILVER money on account of pay, the whole of which the soldier may lay up for himself and friends, as all articles proper for his subsistance and comfort are provided by law, without an espence to him."

Sixty dollars a year was big money because it was to be paid in gold and silver coins, then being exchanged for Continental currency at the rate of about $1 in specie for $40 in currency. Hard work and frugal living for a period of many years wouldn't permit a person to put aside $60 in gold and silver.

But even the rawest country youths didn't rush to recruitment centers because it was universally known that regardless of what the posters might say, George Washington was often unable to pay his fighting men. Reality of army life, contrasted with promises of recruiting parties, helped create a climate that led to bitter criticism and even open mutiny.

Lynch Law

Early in August, 1781, Cornwallis selected Yorktown, Virginia, as temporary headquarters for his army. Size of the force—far too big to be met by any troops that the commonwealth could raise—brought fear and chaos to Virginia. Even in regions such as Bedford County, where patriots were securely in command, it proved difficult or impossible to conform to "due process of law."

Charles Lynch, born at Chestnut Hill plantation near Lynchburg in 1736, had already proved himself a patriot who would be loyal to the end. Lynch had signed the Williamsburg protests of 1769 and 1774, had served in the Virginia constitutional convention of 1776, and sat in the Virginia House of Delegates until early in 1778.

Long before the outbreak of hostilities, some time in 1766, he took the oath of office and became a justice of the peace. It was natural for patriots of Bedford County to turn to Lynch for leadership when loyalists began to engage in raids against the farmhouses of patriots.

With Cornwallis believed to be virtually certain of victory, no matter what Continental force might oppose him, Charles Lynch established an extralegal court to deal with loyalists. Numerous persons popularly labeled "conspirators" were brought before Lynch, who gave most of them a hasty hearing and then pronounced stiff sentences.

Later the Virginia Assembly examined events in Bedford County and concluded that actions of Lynch and his followers were not strictly warranted by law—but were "justifiable from the imminence of the danger." Hasty and often arbitrary decisions by the justice of the peace, not by gangs of vigilantes, established "lynch law" as an American label for trial by ordinary citizens rather than by established courts.

"The World Turned Upside Down"

Reports of eyewitnesses to the British surrender at Yorktown —pivotal moment that meant the beginning of the end for His Majesty's forces in North America—differ in their accounts. All agree that (as was customary) musicians of the defeated body filled the air with sounds while ceremonies proceeded. Most accounts say that British drummers made music, but a few suggest that a full military band was involved.

According to the most widespread accounts, the tune used by the British was "The World Turned Upside Down." Both in England and in the colonies, mothers and nursery maids were accustomed to humming it to lull infants and children to sleep.

In pre-Yorktown days, the opening lines of the ballad referred to a family quarrel:

> Goody Bull and her daughter together fell out.
> Both squabbled, and wrangled, and made a damned rout,
> But the cause of the quarrel remains to be told.
> Then lend both your ears, and a tale I'll unfold.

As published in the *Gentleman's Magazine* in 1766, the ballad about the family quarrel ran to eleven stanzas.

After Yorktown, jubilant Americans wrote numerous sets of words of their own. One of the most popular, still entitled "The World Turned Upside Down," utilized the familiar nursery tune with words that began:

> Cornwallis led a country dance,
>   The like was never seen, sir.
> Much retrograde and much advance,
>   And all with General Greene, sir.

Just why British drummers (or bandsmen) selected a nursery tune as the background for surrender remains an unsolved mystery of the Revolution.

Henry Conway, America's Forgotten Friend

Henry Seymour Conway, younger brother of England's influential Duke of Hertford, had every reason to be a foe of American patriots. Like most younger sons in great families of the era, he entered the army early and was in every sense a professional soldier. By 1756, when he was thirty-five, Conway was a major general.

In spite of his high rank and the fact that it tended to identify him with established power, as a member of Parliament who first took his seat in 1741, he proved to be one of England's most steadfast supporters of the American cause.

As Secretary of State and leader of the House of Commons, it was Conway who first moved in the Cabinet to repeal the Stamp Act. "If we do not," he declared then, "the effect will be to lose the Colonies forever."

His prestige was so great and his military reputation so sound that King George III considered naming him commander in chief of the forces in America. Advisors of the ruler warned him not to make the offer. Conway would reject it, they said, and the British hold upon North America would be weakened as a result.

Unlike Burke and Pitt, Conway never distinguished himself as an orator. But steadily and quietly he espoused the cause of American rights. On December 12, 1781, it was Conway who moved in Parliament that the king be petitioned to stop the American war—a motion lost by just one vote. Two months later, Conway made one of his rare public speeches: proposing a bill that would admit the impossibility of bringing Americans to terms by military force and authorizing a start toward peace negotiations. It was this bill by the quiet-spoken professional soldier that toppled the English Cabinet and eventually ended the Revolutionary War.

Joshua Huddy, Martyr

Instead of subsiding as the war drew toward its inevitable close, friction between patriots and loyalists grew more intense. Sponsored by Lord Henry Clinton fresh from his battlefield victories in the south, loyalists of New York and New Jersey established a formal association. They intended, they said, both to look after their personal interests and to coordinate activity against Whigs and other rebels.

It was in this climate that Philip White of New Jersey took his schooner, the *Wasp*, to Long Branch in Monmouth County. He had been made to forfeit land there, but wanted to take a look at it.

After completing a hasty tour of inspection the loyalist headed back toward his ship. Captured as he neared it, he later tried to escape and was cut down by the sword of Joshua Huddy, a Whig.

To those Americans who had remained loyal to Britain, this was not war, but murder. Captain Richard Lippincott, heading a sixteen-man party of loyalists, took custody of Huddy for the ostensible purpose of transporting him to New York for trial. Instead of doing that, the loyalists dispensed with formalities and hanged Huddy at Gravelly Point, New Jersey, on April 12, 1782.

A placard pinned to the corpse of the martyr read: "We, the refugees, having long with grief beheld the cruel murders of our brethren . . . determine not to suffer without taking vengeance . . . and having made use of Captain Huddy we further determine to hang man for man while there is a refugee existing. *Up goes Huddy for Philip White.*"

Gunboat Diplomacy

British defeats suffered by Admiral Thomas Graves and by General Charles Cornwallis clearly meant the end of British attempts to subdue colonists in North America by force. It was time for hostilities to cease and for a treaty to be formulated.

One enormous stumbling block lay in the way of advocates of peace on both sides of the Atlantic. British pride had been wounded so deeply that it would be hard to persuade delegates to go the peace table even though defeated on the sea and land.

Spring, 1782, brought a surprise victory far from North American shores that served to salve British pride and to create a climate in which independence of the colonies could be recognized without undue humiliation.

No American forces were involved in the clash. French warships under the command of the Comte de Grasse fought with an English fleet headed by Admiral Sir George Rodney. They met in April in waters off the West Indies. Rodney's flagship, the ninety-gun *Formidable,* was no match for the *Ville de Paris,* generally regarded as the biggest and most powerful warship afloat.

These vessels, along with sixty-seven other ships of the line, slugged it out with one another in a running fight that ended in British victory and included capture of de Grasse and his great flagship.

This triumph over Britain's ancient foe had an electric effect upon public opinion. Now that England had once more shown herself to be mistress of the seas, it would not be unduly humiliating to put an end to the "sorry business in the North American colonies." This climate led to peace and to recognition of the independence of the United States by the mother country. Lacking the impact of Rodney's naval victory, diplomats might have dragged their feet for years for fear that U.S. recognition would be too humiliating for Great Britain to endure.

America's First Woman Soldier

Since Robert Surtleiff had no beard, the young soldier's comrades thought up a special nickname: the Blooming Boy. Dressed as a male, the Blooming Boy was actually Deborah Sampson.

Born in Plympton, Massachusetts, on Dec. 17, 1760, she came from a family so poor that she worked as a hired girl. Just before her twenty-first birthday she cut her hair, stole a suit from neighbor Sam Leonard, and volunteered for service in the Continental Army.

Assigned to the 4th Massachusetts Regiment of Foot, the recruit got about ten days of training. Then on June 4, 1782, she marched away to help fight the British. Fellow soldiers had no idea that there was a woman in the ranks of Captain George Webb's company.

"Robert" marched all the way to West Point, then took place in several engagements. Hand to hand fighting brought a sabre slash that the young soldier brushed aside as unimportant in refusing to accept medical treatment.

Then a bullet in the thigh sent Robert to a field hospital. French doctors reluctantly yielded to pleading of the youth and left the wound undressed. In November, 1782, with the wound having healed, Robert went up the Hudson to Ticonderoga. Later, General John Paterson picked him for service as a personal orderly.

In November, 1783, "Robert" was discovered to be Deborah Sampson in disguise—and was promptly mustered out of service. Her lost story was uncovered during World War II, and in tribute to America's first woman soldier a Liberty Ship launched at Baltimore on April 10, 1944, was given her name.

"A Compliment to the King of France"

When Captain Joshua Huddy was hanged by loyalists without the formality of a trial, George Washington set out to even the score. On May 3, 1782, he ordered Brigadier General Moses Hazen to select a British officer to be executed in retaliation.

Hazen was told immediately to designate by lot—or blind choice—"a British Captain who is an unconditional Prisoner, if such a one is in your possession, if not, a Lieutenant." The man so selected was to be sent "under a Safe Guard" to Philadelphia "where the Minister of War will order a proper Guard to receive and conduct him to the place of his Destination."

General Hazen promptly obeyed, and the lot fell upon nineteen-year-old Captain Asgill. Robert R. Livingston, U.S. Secretary for Foreign Affairs, called it "really a melancholy case." Alexander Hamilton spoke far more plainly. Writing to Henry Knox he said that "a sacrifice of this sort is entirely repugnant to the genius of the age we live in, and is without example in modern history, nor can it fail to be considered in Europe as wanton and unnecessary."

Franklin consulted with the commander in chief and reported of Washington that "I am persuaded that nothing I could say to him would have the least effect in changing his determination."

Lady Asgill, mother of the captain, pled the case with every dignitary she could reach. A letter to the French Comte de Vergennes brought results. Writing from Versailles on July 29, 1782, the count told Washington that the king and queen of France begged clemency for Asgill. Transmitted to Congress, the royal request brought a motion that "the life of Capt. Asgill should be given as a compliment to the King of France." It passed unanimously, and the once-doomed officer was escorted to New York and liberated.

Newburgh, New York

Settled about 1708, the town of Newburgh, New York, today appears on no list of major American communities. As a manufacturing and shipping center, it is not greatly different from numerous other centers with population of 30,000 to 40,000.

During 1782-83, however, the town on the Hudson River was George Washington's headquarters. It was here that the Continental Army was formally disbanded.

And though few Americans then or now could pinpoint the spot, it was at Newburgh that the final definitive decision to make this country a democracy was made.

While at Newburgh, George Washington received from Lewis Nicola a famous letter urging him to become king of a new American monarchy. Nicola's sentiments were shared by many patriots, some of whom had a deep and pervasive suspicion of the whole democratic process. Had Washington been sympathetic to the move, he might well have mounted a throne rather than assuming the presidency (in 1789).

It was at obscure little Newburgh that another fateful move was made. Discontented army officers planned a coup that would have led to a military take-over of the infant nation. Alexander Hamilton got wind of the affair in February, 1783. He immediately sent Washington an urgent warning. In spite of the fact that General Horatio Gates was among the malcontents who planned to meet in Newburgh without authorization, the commander in chief put a quick end to the "Newburgh Conspiracy." Unarmed and without an escort of guards, he personally appeared at an officers' meeting on March 15 and persuaded men whom he had led in battle to give up ideas that could have led to military dictatorship as the form of government of the United States.

Some Fighting Slaves Won Freedom

In the various colonies, treatment of slaves who enlisted in the military forces varied widely.

James Robinson of Maryland was told he would be given his freedom if he would fight against the English. He did fight for most of the war, but was rewarded by being taken to Louisiana and sold.

Charlestown Edes of the 15th Massachusetts Regiment signed up as a slave—so regularly authorized the regimental quartermaster to remit his wages to his master, Isaiah Edes of Groton.

Many others were more fortunate, but there is no record of the number of slaves who won their freedom by bearing arms in defense of the young nation. The majority who did so enlisted under false names and passed themselves off as free men, deliberately disappearing from former haunts after hostilities ceased.

An exception involved a slave belonging to Captain Jonathan Hobby of the 3rd Massachusetts Regiment. Convinced that his man had taken up a musket and enlisted in the Continental Army, the military officer took the case to his commander in chief. A search conducted through official channels would turn up the missing slave, he insisted.

Hobby was notified that a Court of Inquiry would look into the case. But he never recovered the runaway slave. On February 2, 1783, George Washington notified General Rufus Putnam that "the Commander in Chief does not think himself authorized to discharge the Sd Negro, unless another man is obtained by the State, or otherwise, to serve in his room." Captain Hobby, who got a copy of the decision a few days later, realized that it would be impossible to secure a replacement for the black soldier who had found a haven in the army, so the case was dropped.

Terrible Toll of Dead and Wounded

Evacuation of Long Island and Staten Island by the British on December 4, 1783, convinced even the last lingering doubters that the war was over. Exulting at the great victory, an anonymous pamphleteer of the day bewailed the "terrible toll of dead and wounded" Americans.

Actually, the Revolution from start to finish involved far fewer casualties than individual battles of later eras. Statistics are less than fully reliable. In some cases, they amount to estimates—but the same variable applies to other wars.

As reported in the *World Almanac,* the Continental Army suffered 4,435 battle deaths during the Revolution. Only 342 members of the Continental Navy were officially listed as killed in action—and the Marines lost just 49. An additional 6,188 soldiers, sailors, and marines suffered wounds that were not fatal.

Battlefield deaths in the Civil War ran to 140,414 among Union forces and 74,524 among Confederates. There never was even an estimate of nonfatal wounds among Confederates, but the men in blue reported 281,881 such wounds.

World War I was less costly in men than was the Civil War; it took only about thirteen times as many American lives as did the Revolution. But the toll in World War II (battle deaths) ran to 292,131.

Even Viet Nam made the entire American Revolution seem like a single big skirmish in terms of casualties. For every patriot who died in order to help free his country from British rule, approximately fourteen died in Southeast Asia.

Benjamin Franklin's Tory Son

Long after hostilities ended, scars remained. A little-known letter from Benjamin Franklin to the Reverend Dr. Byles of Boston, written on the first day of 1788, indicates how deep and how strong the emotional currents actually were.

"My son is estranged from me by the part he took in the late war, and keeps aloof," Franklin wrote. "The part he acted against me, which is of public notoriety, will account for my leaving him no more of an estate he endeavored to deprive me of."

Until middle life Benjamin Franklin's son William (1731-1813) was the apple of his father's eye. He was the natural son of the Sage of Philadelphia, probably by Franklin's common-law wife Deborah Read.

As a boy, William was fond of books. Later he entered military service and became a captain in the Pennsylvania forces at eighteen. In the famous kite experiment of 1752, when lightning was shown to be a form of electricity, it was Billy who assisted his father. At the time he was twenty-one—not the adolescent boy usually depicted—and won an M.A. degree from Oxford University for his role in the experiment. It was for Billy that his father began writing his famous *Autobiography*.

But when war broke out, William parted company with his father in order to remain a loyal subject of England. While on a journey to England in 1762 he had been named royal governor of New Jersey—and refused to give up his post at his father's urging. Governor Franklin was declared "an enemy to the liberties of this country" on June 15, 1776, and arrested shortly afterward. Though he later tried to attempt a reconciliation, his famous father remained aloof—and in his will cut him off with a token bequest.

Patrick Henry vs. the Constitution

Once the Constitution of the United States was written, it promised what patriots had wanted from the start—a unified nation rather than a loose confederation of independent colonies. But before the document could become law, it needed the ratification of nine states. Eight acted promptly and decisively.

Debate in the Virginia legislature began on June 2, 1788, with Patrick Henry the chief spokesman against ratification. The issue was crucial, for if Virginia rejected the document most or all other Southern states were likely to follow. If Virginia voted ratification, the issue was settled. James Madison was strongly in favor of immediate favorable action; so was John Marshall, along with a host of less notable leaders.

Patrick Henry put everything he had into fervent opposition to ratification. His public attacks were based chiefly on the fact that the proposed national charter included no bill of rights (long ago accepted in England).

"If you pass this paper without a Bill of Rights," he told fellow Virginians in one of several impassioned speeches, "you will exhibit the most absurd thing the world ever saw: a government [the state of Virginia] that has abandoned all its power—the powers of the purse, the sword and the press without check, limitation or control."

Henry continued his fight for twenty-three days, to his chagrin saw the Virginia Legislature vote for ratification of the U.S. Constitution on June 25, 1788, with eighty-nine votes "Aye" and seventy-nine "Nay." History proved his stand to be prophetic, however, for many of the earliest amendments were aimed at providing remedies for defects that the Virginian had emphasized.

Bibliography

Literature produced during and centering upon the American Revolution is so vast that only the most important sources of this volume can be listed. Many (but not all) of the persons, places, and events treated briefly in these pages are themselves subjects of entire books.

Adams, James Truslow. *The Epic of America*. Boston: Atlantic-Little, Brown, 1931.

Almon, John, ed., *The Parliamentary Register*. London: J. Almon, 1775-84.

American Heritage, Vols. 1-24.

American History Illustrated, Vols. 1-7. (See especially "The Concise Illustrated History of the American Revolution." April, 1972.)

Andrews, Charles M. *The Colonial Background of the American Revolution*. New Haven, Conn.: Yale University Press, 1924.

The Annual Register, or a View of the History, Politics, and Literature (for the Years 1775, 1776, 1777, 1778, 1779, 1780, 1781, 1782). London: J. Dodsley, 1776-83.

Bancroft, George. *History of the United States*. Boston: Little, Brown, 1874.

Becker, Carl L. *The Eve of the Revolution*. New Haven, Conn.: Yale University Press, 1921.

Bigelow, John, ed. *Benjamin Franklin, Complete Works*. New York: Putnam, 1887-89.

Boyd, Julian P., ed. *The Papers of Thomas Jefferson*. Princeton, N. J.: Princeton University Press, 1950-60.

Burnett, Edmund C. *The Continental Congress*. New York: Macmillan, 1942.

Commager, Henry S., and Morris, Richard, eds. *The Spirit of 'Seventy-Six*. New York: Bobbs-Merrill, 1958.

Demis, Samuel F. *The Diplomacy of the American Revolution*. New York: Appleton-Century, 1935.

Johnson, Allen, ed. *Dictionary of American Biography*. New York: Scribner's, 1928.

Adams, James Truslow, ed. *Dictionary of American History*. New York: Scribner's 1940-61.

Stephen, Leslie and Lee, Sidney, eds. *Dictionary of National Biography*. London: Smith, Elder & Co., 1908-9.

Egerton, H. E. *The Causes and Character of the American Revolution*. Oxford: Oxford University Press, 1923.

Fitzpatrick, John C., ed. *The Diaries of George Washington, 1748-99*. Boston: Houghton Mifflin, 1925.

———. *The Writings of George Washington*. Washington: U. S. Government Printing Office, 1931-44.

Gabriel, Ralph H., ed. *The Pageant of America*. New Haven, Conn.: Yale University Press, 1926-29.

Gipson, Lawrence H. *The British Empire Before the American Revolution*. Caldwell, Idaho: Caxton Printers, 1939.

Hunt, Gaillard, ed. *The Writings of James Madison*. New York: Putnam's, 1900-1909.

Hutchinson, Thomas, ed. *Diary and Letters of Thomas Hutchinson*. Boston: Houghton, 1884-86.

Jefferson, Thomas. *Notes on the State of Virginia*. New York: Putnam's, 1894.

Ketchum, Richard M. *The Winter Soldiers*. Garden City, N. Y.: Doubleday, 1973.

Lancaster, Bruce. *From Lexington to Liberty*. Garden City, N.Y.: Doubleday, 1955.

Lecky, W. E. H. *The American Revolution*. New York: Appleton-Century, 1939.

————. *History of England in the Eighteenth Century.* New York: Appleton, 1883.

Mahan, A. T. *The Influence of Sea Power upon History.* Rev. ed. Boston: Little [1897], 1902

Miller, John C. *Triumph of Freedom.* Boston: Little, Brown, 1948.

Morison, S. E. and Commager, H. S. *The Growth of the American Republic.* New York: Oxford University Press, 1937.

Morris, Richard B. *The Era of the American Revolution.* New York: Columbia University Press, 1939.

Namier, L. B. *England in the Age of the American Revolution.* London: Macmillan, 1930.

Nevins, Allan, *The American States During and After the Revolution.* New York: Macmillan, 1924.

Osgood, H. L. *The American Colonies in the Eighteenth Century.* New York: Columbia University Press, 1924.

Ramsay, David. *History of the American Revolution.* London: Stockdale, 1793.

Ross, Charles, ed. *Correspondence of Cornwallis.* London: Murray, 1859.

Smyth, Albert H. ed. *The Writings of Benjamin Franklin.* New York: Macmillan, 1905-07.

Stevens, Benjamin Franklin. *B. F. Stevens' Facsimiles of Manuscripts in European Archives Relating to America, 1773-1783.* London: Malby & Sons, 1889-1895.

Stryker, William S. *The Battles of Trenton and Princeton.* Boston: Houghton, Mifflin, 1898.

Thane, Elswyth. *The Family Quarrel.* New York: Duell, Sloan & Pearce; 1959.

Van Doren, Carl. *Secret History of the American Revolution.* New York: Viking Press, 1941.

Van Tyne, Claude H. *The Loyalists in the American Revolution.* New York: Peter Smith, 1929.

Walpole, Horace. *Journal of the Reign of George III from 1771 to 1783.* London: Bentley, 1859.

Wharton, Francis, ed. *The Revolutionary Diplomatic Correspondence of the United States.* Washington: U. S. Government Printing Office, 1889.

Index

172